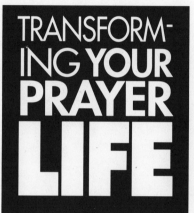

TRANSFORM-ING YOUR PRAYER LIFE

WITHDRAWN

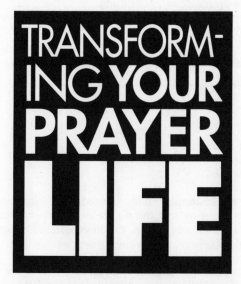

TRANSFORMING YOUR PRAYER LIFE

A SEVEN-WEEK STRATEGY TO A MORE MEANINGFUL RELATIONSHIP WITH GOD

Dr. Bob Beltz

Wolgemuth & Hyatt, Publishers, Inc.
Brentwood, Tennessee

The mission of Wolgemuth & Hyatt, Publishers, Inc. is to publish and distribute books that lead individuals toward:

- A personal faith in the one true God: Father, Son, and Holy Spirit;

- A lifestyle of practical discipleship; and

- A worldview that is consistent with the historic, Christian faith.

Moreover, the Company endeavors to accomplish this mission at a reasonable profit and in a manner which glorifies God and serves His Kingdom.

Wolgemuth & Hyatt, Publishers, Inc.
1749 Mallory Lane, Suite 110
Brentwood, Tennessee 37027

Library of Congress Cataloging-in-Publication Data

Beltz, Bob.
    Transforming your prayer life : a seven-week strategy to a more
meaningful relationship with God / Bob Beltz.
        p. cm.
    Includes index.
    ISBN 1-56121-088-9
    1. Prayer. 2. Lord's prayer. 3. Spiritual exercises. I. Title.
BV215.B42 1990
248.3'2—dc20   91-3906
                                                                      CIP

To Allison: wife, lover, friend, and life partner: "Many women have done nobly, but you excel them all!" (Proverbs 31:29, NASB)

CONTENTS

ACKNOWLEDGMENTS

I would like to express my deep appreciation to the men and women who have made this book possible. First, I am eternally grateful to Rich Beach for the role he has played in my life as a spiritual father, mentor, and friend. My partner in ministry, Jim Dixon, has been a constant source of encouragement and affirmation throughout the sixteen years we have labored together in the ministry. Without his support, this book could never have been written.

I am deeply indebted to Diane Rutter for her sacrificial work in typing the manuscript. Without her loving labor the book would still be a pile of yellow legal pads hidden somewhere in the chaos that covers the top of my desk. As always, Judy Fields's administrative assistance was invaluable during the actual writing of the book.

A great big "Thanks!" must go to the elders of Cherry Hills Community Church who granted the sabbatical which enabled me to write. Finally, I am immensely grateful for the men and women of "The Company of the Committed" who not only endured the teaching of the material contained within these pages, but actually acted like they enjoyed it! To all of you, I say, "Thanks!"

INTRODUCTION

T he purpose of this book is to help you learn to pray more effectively and consistently. Actually, there is only one way to learn how to pray. We learn to pray by praying. Many of us have read books on prayer, listened to tapes on prayer, and studied prayer, yet we don't pray.

So what makes this book different from the rest? Rather than trying to teach you to pray, I hope to be a coach and cheerleader who encourages you while you actually begin to pray. I hope to share some ideas and strategies with you that have helped to transform my prayer life.

Over the years I have known people (very few, I must admit) who seem to have a special gift for prayer. It seems to come naturally for them. They spend hours in prayer. I have envied those people for years. Prayer has been hard for me. What I share in this book comes from the perspective of a fellow struggler. But I have good news for you. By the grace of God and by the power of the Spirit, we can become men and women of prayer!

All over the world today there is a grass roots movement toward more significant prayer. I believe this is a movement of the Spirit of God leading men and women into lives of more effective and effectual prayer. We live in an exciting moment of history. This kind of movement has historically preceded great spiritual awakenings. During these periods of awakening, the entire fabric of society (usually in a state of decline—morally, ethically, and spiritually) has been changed. It seems as if God is preparing a foundation of prayer for what He wants to do in this decade. He is calling forth the church to be a body of men and women who pray.

Charles Finney once observed, "We have had instruction until we are hardened. It's now time for us to pray." That is certainly true for the church today. The time has come: let's begin to pray!

WEEK ONE:

EXPLORING YOUR MOTIVATION

One

THE NEED

Y ou would think it would have become an embarrassment much sooner. How many times in nearly twenty years had I responded to inquiries concerning my personal spiritual life with a statement like, "It's going great *but* I really need to work on my prayer life"? For almost twenty years I had maintained the discipline of a daily (well, almost daily) quiet time. I had always found time to read and study the Bible as well as time to read a small library of good Christian books. I had completed both a master's degree and a doctorate in pastoral ministry. I had even been working in full-time Christian ministry for nearly eighteen years, and yet my prayer life was still not what I knew it needed to be.

ONE MAN'S FRUSTRATION

In his excellent little booklet, *Tyranny of the Urgent,* Charles E. Hummel quotes P. T. Forsythe's conviction that "the worst sin is prayerlessness." Don't get me wrong. My life was not prayerless. I had always spent some time daily in prayer. I had even built a small history of exciting answers to prayer. I enjoyed seasons of more intensive prayer. I had even spent half days and whole days in prayer. But I had never been able to develop a consistent, effective, satisfying prayer discipline. That situation has changed, and the change is my motivation for sharing these ideas with you. If you desire to be a man or woman of prayer and if you are willing to follow the simple game plan this book will develop for you, you can transform your prayer life with a very simple plan.

THE PRAYERLESS CHURCH

Over the years, as I have struggled with this area of my relationship with God, it has become apparent to me that I am not alone. As a matter of fact, the usual response to my confession of inadequacy in my prayer life has often been an empathetic "Me, too!" At the turning point in my own experience, the pervasiveness of this tragedy within the evangelical sector of the church was driven home to me.

In April 1989, I attended a conference on prayer led by John Wimber of the Vineyard Ministries. At that conference, John shared the results of recent research concerning prayer within the evangelical church. The findings of this research indicate that the average "born-again," Bible-believing, evangelical Christian spends less than four minutes a day in prayer. I believe that statistic actually might be optimistic. John also shared that the same study revealed that the average "born-again," Bible-believing, evangelical Christian *pastor* spends an average of less than eight minutes a day in prayer.

While I don't want to sound legalistic or pharisaic, let me make the observation that, if these statistics are true, we have a prayerless evangelical church. This seems to be something of a contradiction in terms, but I fear it is true.

*"The average 'born-again,'
Bible-believing, evangelical
Christian pastor spends less than
eight minutes a day in prayer."*

THE WINDS OF CHANGE

In light of what appears to be a rather dismal picture, I must say that I am actually encouraged—obviously not by the past state of affairs, but by what I see happening at a grass roots level all around our country. I believe the winds of change are blowing. I think something is up, and I have a hunch that God is behind it. I believe my own experience is the same as that of many men and women within the body of Christ. A new commitment to a life of more consistent and effective prayer is being blessed by a touch of God's Spirit. This touch is enabling people to respond to the call to pray with a new level of conviction and excitement. Simply put, a transformation is taking place in the prayer lives of multitudes of men and women. This same transformation can happen to you!

A PERSONAL PILGRIMAGE

In my own life, I find that I usually end up doing the things I am highly motivated to do. For a follower of Christ, obedience should be a sufficient reason to pray. I would have to say that whatever caliber of prayer life I have maintained over the last twenty years has been motivated by obedience. The obvious problem I encountered was that the quality of prayer produced by the motivation of obedience was inadequate. Knowing our hearts, God has other ways to motivate us if He sees sufficient willingness and desire lying dormant within us. For me, that motivation came through a series of unlikely channels.

This Present Darkness

As a pastor in a large and dynamic church filled with wonderful, caring, and sharing people, I am always being given books that someone assures me I *have* to read. But, as a pastor in a large and dynamic church filled with wonderful, caring, and sharing people, my schedule and limited supply of physical, spiritual, and emotional energy keep me from reading many of those books. So I consider it a work of grace that God made sure that one of the books I did read was Frank Perretti's *This Present Darkness.*

The book is a novel about the reality of the unseen universe and how the unseen universe is constantly impinging on the seen universe. At one level, the plot line unfolds the drama of events occurring in the fictional town of Ashton. Strange and bizarre changes are occurring in Ashton. The moral and ethical environment of the community is deteriorating. The small college in Ashton is being infiltrated by professors who advocate strange, New Age-type metaphysical beliefs and practices. In general, unhealthy dynamics are growing in the community.

While the story develops along these lines, a second level of reality is introduced. The genius of *This Present Darkness* lies in Perretti's ability to portray the reality of what the Bible calls the "principalities" and "powers" of the heavenly realm (Ephesians 6:1). The book lets us "see" the unseen. Over the little town of Ashton, spiritual warfare is being waged. The host of heaven is in conflict with the spiritual faces of evil. The temporal effects in the lives of the citizens of Ashton and the events transpiring in the city are the by-products of this war in heaven.

The most significant message of the book, however, lies in the fact that the outcome of the war in heaven lies in the hands of a remnant of men and women in Ashton. In a little church in Ashton, a small group of men and women begin to pray for their city. As these men and women pray, the power of the host of heaven is increased. When they fail to pray, the demonic forces of evil prevail. Whether or not you agree with the theology of the novel (and it *is* just a novel), one truth is clearly communicated. The prayers of God's people are effectual in influencing heavenly realities. We must also remember that those heavenly realities will influence earthly realities. Prayer not only influences the work; to a great degree, prayer *is* the work.

As it did for multitudes of people around our country, *This Present Darkness* rekindled my spiritual desire to become a more effective man of prayer. I had the desire; now I needed a strategy to turn that desire into action.

Teach Us to Pray

My strategy came through a series of events that ultimately led me to the most obvious strategy imaginable. Because of my motivation to learn to pray more effectively, I was a sure candidate for a conference that came to our city. The conference was entitled "Teach Us to Pray." It was hosted by one of the Vineyard fellowships in our town and was being taught by John Wimber, the leader of the Vineyard movement, a dynamic, charismatic ministry out of southern California.

You need to remember that I am an ordained Presbyterian minister, trained in a very traditional evangelical framework. Many in my circle of experience and theology view the thought of attending a conference taught by John as borderline taboo. But having close friends who are involved in the Vineyard movement and having personally profited from much of what the movement has brought to the body of Christ, I felt relatively safe going to this conference on prayer.

Ironically, after spending an entire week at the conference, I was a bit frustrated by the fact that John never got to the subject of how to pray. He spent most of the week focusing on why we need to pray in light of what he believed to be a prophetic picture of the coming decade. In the course of the week, he did make one statement that had a tremendous impact on my life. John said he was indebted to Larry Lea of the Church on the Rock for Larry's influence on his prayer life. John pointed out that, even though he and Larry were not in complete theological agreement, he was indebted to the model of prayer Larry practiced and Larry's discipleship in prayer. At the time I didn't think much about the comment, but as is so common in the way the Lord works, it was pivotal in what God was about to do for me.

Could You Not Tarry One Hour?

Monday morning after the conference, I was back at work in my office. I called one of the women on our staff to set up a meeting. She informed me that she was listening to a really great series of tapes on prayer by guess whom? Larry Lea! I asked if I could borrow them. Through this series of unlikely events, God gave me the strategy I needed.

The series of tapes is called "Could You Not Tarry One Hour?" In the first tape, Dr. Lea takes his listeners back to that moment in the Garden of Gethsemane when Jesus asked His disciples this question. At the most critical hour of His life, Jesus took His three closest disciples aside and asked them to "tarry" with Him while He prayed. You know the scene. Jesus prayed; the disciples slept. When Jesus discovered that they were asleep, He asked this question: "Could you not tarry one hour?"

I began to realize that, in a sense, the question Jesus was asking the disciples was, "Could you not pray?" I began to have the uneasy feeling that if my present discipline of prayer were to continue, that might be the question Jesus

> *"I decided to wake up! I resolved that by the grace of God and with the help of the Holy Spirit, I would begin to pray. I didn't mean the four or five minutes a day I had been praying. I decided to learn to pray for an hour."*

would ask me when I entered His presence. I had been "sleeping." That day I made an important commitment. I decided to wake up! I resolved that by the grace of God and with the help of the Holy Spirit, I would begin to pray. I didn't mean the four or five minutes a day I had been praying. I decided to learn to pray for an hour. I meant it—and I did something about it! I linked my motivation to a commitment. Then I added action to my commitment.

That day, I looked at my watch and I prayed, "Holy Spirit, help me pray for fifteen minutes today." Do you know what happened? I prayed for fifteen minutes. It was actually easy and joyful. The next day I prayed, "Holy Spirit, help me pray for thirty minutes." I prayed using a pattern based on the Lord's Prayer. When I finished praying, I looked at my watch. Thirty minutes had gone by. The next day I asked for forty-five minutes and got it. Finally, four days into my new commitment, I prayed for one solid hour!

I know the dangers that some of you might be listing. This might sound like legalism to some. To others it might sound self-righteous. I know those dangers exist. But my hunch is that, for most of us, prayerlessness is a much greater problem than either legalism or self-righteousness.

That week marked the beginning of an exciting journey for me. I began to have what I believe is an exciting and significant prayer life. I don't always pray for an hour, and I don't always get a significant block of prayer every day. But I can tell you this: the prayer dimension of my relationship with Christ has been transformed.

YOUR PRAYER LIFE

Let me ask you a very important question. How is *your* prayer life? If it is great—if it is satisfying, effective, and productive—you probably don't need to read this book. Give it to a friend. But, if you are struggling with this area of your spiritual life, this book is for you!

Here is the good news. Prayer does not come naturally for me. If I began to pray, you can begin to pray! If you will follow the simple instructions and assignments in this book, I believe your prayer life will be transformed, and so will your relationship with Christ. Are you sick and tired of being sick and tired? Are you ready to do what it takes to begin to pray? Then let me challenge you right now to make the following commitment:

Father, by your grace and with your help, I resolve this _____ day of _____ in the year _____ to become a man/woman of prayer.

Signed: _____

WEEK ONE:

DEVELOPING A STRATEGY

Two

"TEACH US TO PRAY"

For twenty years, I have attempted to follow Jesus Christ. During these years, I have struggled with the tension that seems to exist between relying on the power of God to accomplish His purposes in my life and the need for my own effort and discipline. This, I believe, is certainly the dilemma many men and women face as they pray. How much does an effective prayer life depend on my discipline and how much on God's grace?

I believe the biblical answer to that question is found in Philippians 2:12–13:

> Therefore, my dear friends, as you have always obeyed—not only in my presence, but now much more in my absence—continue to work out your salvation with fear and trembling, for it is God who works in you to will and to act according to his good purpose.

This text tells us that progress in our walk with Christ is a combination of what God does and what we do. God *is* at work *in* you. He is the great motivator, enabler, and empowerer. But what God is working within needs to be worked out by our actions of obedience. The formula I have come up with is simple. God's work in and through our lives requires

—— WILL POWER ——

Not in the normal sense of those words. Biblical willpower involves the exercise of my will to act, combined with dependence upon God's power to enable. The formula looks like this:

—— MY WILL + HIS POWER ——

In almost every facet of spiritual life, we will find this to be the simple answer. It is the formula of the beloved hymn "Trust and Obey." I must trust Him for motivation, enabling, and empowerment; but I must then step out in faith and obey.

In developing a discipline of prayer, the first step is to come to the Lord as the disciples did and to ask Him to teach us to pray. I am sure that, by the time the disciples made this request, they had spent quite a bit of time and energy trying to pray. They were all good Jewish boys and had "known" how to pray since their youth. Is it possible that they were feeling as frustrated as you and I in their efforts?

One day Jesus Christ invaded their lives, and they saw a model that challenged their conceptions of prayer. Jesus was always praying! Sometimes, they woke up in the morning and He was gone. Where? He had risen a great while before dawn and gone off to pray (Mark 1:35). Other times, He prayed all night (Luke 6:12). Sometimes, He sent the disciples on to their next destination while He remained behind to pray (Matthew 14:23). Finally, one day He was praying, we are told, "in a certain place," and they had seen enough. "Teach us to pray," they asked (Luke 11:1).

I would like to suggest that perhaps they came to a recognition that their prayer lives were deficient. Theirs certainly didn't resemble Jesus'. Maybe they had even given up on their own ability to pray. Now they were ready to learn.

In response to the disciples' request, Jesus taught them a pattern of prayer that has come to be known as the Lord's Prayer. It would be more accurate to call this pattern "the

---

"In developing a discipline of prayer, the first step is to come to the Lord as the disciples did and to ask Him to teach us to pray."

---

disciple's prayer," given to the disciples by Christ to help them make their experience of prayer more productive and effective.

The "experts" disagree about the intention of this prayer. Some believe it was given as a form prayer to be used liturgically and repetitively. Those who hold such a view claim that the use of liturgical form prayer was common among the rabbis of Jesus' day.

Others believe that the prayer was intended to be a pattern, or outline, that gave the disciples a guide in terms of areas or topics to pray through. Those who believe this to be the case will also claim that the pattern approach to prayer was common among the rabbis of Jesus' day. They will also point to the passage in Matthew 6 where the Lord's Prayer is preceded by a warning against the vain, repetitive prayers of the "pagans" (Matthew 6:7).

THE STRATEGY

In my life, the pattern approach was the very strategy I needed to launch the transformation of my prayer life. I had the motivation. The motivation was even linked with my commitment. I began to take action. All I lacked was a strategy to make my motivated, commitment-based action effective. Using the Lord's Prayer as a pattern of seven topics provided that strategy.

I am convinced that, for many people, this strategy would make prayer relevant and exciting. Many Christians are convinced that prayer is one of the most important dynamics of spiritual life. Pastors like me have repeatedly browbeaten them about their need to pray. They are convinced. They are motivated. They are committed. But they don't know how and what to pray. Once you see how to develop each topic of the Lord's Prayer into one component of your prayer time, you will have the strategy you need to launch the transformation of your prayer life.

SEVEN COMPONENTS OF PRAYER

I love teaching through the life of Christ. While teaching the Gospels I have often analyzed the components of the Lord's Prayer. My problem has been that, having analyzed the components, I failed to develop them adequately in my own prayer times. Listening to Dr. Lea helped me see how rich and full each component in this great prayer can be. Once we begin to develop these areas, I believe we will see how exciting and significant prayer can be.

The pattern Jesus gives has seven components. These components form the framework for Prayer 101. In the following chapters, I will attempt to develop each component to give you an idea of how to incorporate it into your own prayer time.

Component One: Entering His Presence—"Father"

Prayer is preeminently communication with God. In the first component, Jesus tells us to address God as "Father." Immediately our minds should shift to thinking about our relationship with God and what we need to concentrate on as we enter His presence. I use this time to appropriate the helping ministry of the Holy Spirit in prayer.

"Many Christians are convinced that prayer is one of the most important dynamics of spiritual life. . . . They are convinced. They are motivated. They are committed. But they don't know how and what to pray."

Component Two: Seeking His Face—"Hallowed Be Your Name"

Having entered into the presence of God in prayer, Jesus instructs us to spend time hallowing the name of God. The primary focus of prayer is God Himself. I am personally convinced so few men and women have exciting and effective prayer lives because most people focus their prayers on themselves instead of on God. This component enables us to incorporate worship into our prayer time.

The name of God expresses the character of God. The nature and character of God reveal the face of God. During this time of praise and thanksgiving, our minds and hearts are tuned in to God and His agenda. For me, this component of prayer has become one of the most exciting and enjoyable.

Component Three: Appropriating Divine Intervention—"Thy Kingdom Come, Thy Will Be Done"

Having basked in the glory of God as we have sought His face, we now are ready to do some prayer work. As a third component of significant prayer, Jesus extends to us the invitation to appropriate divine intervention. Although there is certainly an eschatological (ask your pastor what that means!) dimension to this component, there is also an immediate application. During this portion of our prayer time, we will seek to bring heavenly realities to bear on earthly situations.

How desperately we need to take advantage of the opportunity Jesus gives us in this component! We need the realities of the kingdom of God to come to bear on our families, our churches, our cities, our nation, and our world. We must learn to exercise the authority given to us to pray for the will of God to be accomplished in all these arenas. This is an exciting and critically important time in prayer!

Component Four: Praying for Provision—"Give Us This Day Our Daily Bread"

Not until this fourth component is reached does our focus shift from God's agenda to our agenda. This seems consistent with the teaching of Christ. Our Father knows our needs and desires to meet them. He only wants our desires to be subordinate to His kingdom. "Seek first his kingdom and his righteousness, and all these things will be given to you as well" (Matthew 6:33). Having sought first the King and the agenda of His kingdom in prayer, we now present our petitions in His presence.

In this component of the "disciples' prayer," Jesus invites us to ask for our daily needs. He provides the opportunity for us to pray through two sets of agendas. First, we can set our day before the throne of God and ask for His touch and His provision on every expectation for it. Second, it can be a time of praying about our concerns that fall more into the category of want than the category of need. Whatever is on our hearts and minds, we now bring to God.

Component Five: Experiencing Forgiveness—"Forgive Us Our Sins, as We Forgive Those Who Sin Against Us"

I am a sinner in constant need of the grace and forgiveness of God. I know that God knows these facts and, as incomprehensible as it seems, loves me anyway. He has provided forgiveness for my sins in Jesus Christ. In confession, I can honestly face God with my failure. And I can experience His forgiveness and His cleansing.

Because we live in a fallen world, we are often the object of someone else's sin. As a result, we can harbor bitterness and resentment against other men and women. We need to work through those destructive attitudes in prayer. This fifth component reminds me that, as I experience Christ's forgiveness in my life, I need to dispense that forgiveness to those who have offended me.

Component Six: Spiritual Protection—"Lead Us Not into Temptation . . . Deliver Us from Evil"

In the sixth chapter of the New Testament book of Ephesians, the Apostle Paul reminds us that "we do not wrestle against flesh and blood, but against principalities, against powers" (Ephesians 6:12, NKJV). Jesus certainly knew the reality of spiritual warfare in His own life. Therefore, He instructs us to set a time aside in our prayer life to pray for spiritual protection.

We are instructed to pray in two areas for spiritual protection. First, Jesus tells us to pray about our own susceptibility to temptation. Second, He tells us to pray for protection from the evil one.

Component Seven: Final Issues—"Yours Is The Kingdom, and the Power, and the Glory, Forever!"

The seventh, and final, component of the pattern is a closing time of praise and affirmation. After we move through all the dimensions of prayer in this pattern, it is appropriate to bring our prayer time to a close with the declaration that in fact our Father is the King and the kingdom is His. We also affirm that all true spiritual power belongs to God and has been made available to us through the Holy Spirit. Finally, we end where we started by giving God the glory due Him.

In one short lesson, Jesus taught the disciples an incredibly effective and thorough pattern of prayer. What I hope to show you in the coming chapters is how to develop each of these components into a more comprehensive strategy for developing a significant prayer life. If you made your commitment to become a man or woman of prayer, get ready to start an exciting adventure!

ASSIGNMENT: WEEK ONE

1. Read Matthew 6:5–15; Luke 11:1–13; Romans 8:26–27.

2. Renew the commitment you made at the end of chapter 1.

3. Outline the seven components of the Lord's Prayer on a sheet of paper.

4. Turn to Appendix B at the end of this book. Notice how each page represents one component of your outline.

5. Ask the Holy Spirit to help you pray five minutes a day, five days this week.

6. Using your outline, pray!

WEEK TWO:

ENTERING HIS PRESENCE

Three

"FATHER"

I have a hole in my soul. It is the nagging source of much of my inner pain and struggle. This wound was caused by the lack of a stable, loving, and nurturing relationship with my father.

DADS

I don't have many conscious memories of my early childhood. The memories I do have of my dad are mixed. I remember some good times with him. I have a few memories of playing catch in the yard and of his help in learning to throw a football and catch a baseball. In later years, I remember his showing up to watch my games when I played football and ran track. Those are some of the good memories.

I remember a lot of painful times with Dad, too. I remember that he had a very difficult time keeping a job. I remember overhearing him and Mom fight about Dad losing his job and Mom having to support us. I remember times when he exploded in fits of rage and how I wanted to hide in my room and cover my ears until the explosion settled down.

I don't remember the day Mom and I left to go live with my grandparents. I was eleven. That was one of the hardest years of my life. An eleven-year-old boy really needs a dad!

I remember Dad coming to visit us in St. Louis and how excited I was when I found out Mom and Dad were going to try again. I remember how it didn't work out too well and how a year later Mom told me she was going to get a divorce. I remember the humiliation of Dad sleeping on an army cot in the garage. I don't remember the day he left for good. I do remember that I never had a normal relationship with him again.

Years later, my wife and I visited Dad in California. He hadn't been able to make it to our wedding. We had a pretty good visit, but it was still kind of sad. I remember the morning in 1978 when the phone rang and my sister told me Dad was dead. I remember when the shock wore off and the tears came. I'm not sure who the grief was really for. I had a sense that I had lost forever something I never really had.

The absence of a loving, caring, and nurturing relationship with a healthy, caring father has taken its toll on my life. There is a hole in my soul. Mom was there to meet the physical needs a parent should take care of. She tried to be both a mom and a dad. Even so, the years have shown that I lost a great deal because of his absence.

The need for a caring, nurturing father is foundational for emotional and spiritual development. I see that clearly now that I am a father myself. Children need a dad who is there for them. They need a dad who cares and nurtures. Their little love tanks need to be filled daily. They need a dad they can count on.

A small child with the same need still lives in each of us. The truth is that our need for a dad will never fully be met by any human father. To one degree or another, all earthly fathers will let us down and disappoint us. Most families have some degree of dysfunction. We are all fallen. But a solution to our problem does exist.

We were created to relate to God as our heavenly Father. He is a perfect Father. He is always present and available. He is loving, caring, and nurturing. He is committed to meeting

---

"The need for a caring, nurturing father is foundational for emotional and spiritual development. . . . We were created to relate to God as our heavenly Father."

---

the physical, emotional, and spiritual needs of our lives. No time in our day is more significant than the time we spend with Him. He is there to fill the hole in our soul.

As I began to use the Lord's Prayer as a pattern for my prayer life, the fatherhood of God began to come alive in my life. I began to realize that, even though I confessed and affirmed that God was now my Father through my relationship with Christ, I had very little experience of that truth in my life. In talking to and with many other men and women about this issue, I find this to be a common dilemma. Most of us need a vehicle whereby the theological truth of the fatherhood of God becomes real in our experience. This is why it is so exciting that the first component of our prayer strategy grows from the teaching of Jesus that we should begin our prayer by addressing God as "our Father." Authentic prayer is an expression of this father-child relationship.

"OUR FATHER"

For many of us, addressing God as "Father" seems like normative behavior. We should realize that this was not the case in Jesus' day. A quick trip through the great prayers of the Old Testament reveals that even the most holy men of the old covenant did not address their prayers to God as "Father."

I recently finished rereading the Old Testament. In this reading, I was particularly interested in the prayers of God's people. The Old Testament holds some powerful and moving prayers. Many of the psalms are beautiful prayers of King David. Notice how David addressed God in prayer. Sometimes he prayed, "Oh, God." Sometimes it was "Oh, Lord." At times of special intimacy he prayed, "Oh, *my* God" or "Oh, *my* Lord." But nowhere will you find David addressing the living God as "Father."

Daniel was also a man of prayer. His prayer life was so powerful that the angel Gabriel was sent to respond personally to Daniel's great prayer recorded in chapter 9 of the book of Daniel. Yet, he did not address God as "Father."

The patriarchs, the prophets, and the priests of Israel were all men of prayer. But you will find no instance of prayers addressed to God as "Father." That privilege is uniquely ours because of who Jesus Christ is and what He has done on our behalf. He has given us the right to become children of God through our relationship with Him, and He has instructed us to begin our prayer with a focus on God as Father.

GETTING STARTED

By beginning our prayer time this way, we start praying within the framework of a father-child dialogue. Our initial focus is on God, our heavenly Father, and on *our relationship* with Him. I think of this time as a period of what I call *preliminaries* to get spiritually prepared for a meaningful and significant time of prayer. For me, this means working through several factors.

First, I acknowledge my inability to pray; and I ask for the promised ministry of the Holy Spirit to help me. I might begin by praying something like this:

> Father, I would like to spend some time today with You in prayer. You know that I don't know how to pray or have the ability to pray in a way that is pleasing to You and significant for me. Therefore I ask the Holy Spirit to help me pray as Your Word promises that He will. (see Romans 8:26–27)

I get very specific about my need for help. If I want to have an hour of prayer, I ask the Holy Spirit to help me pray for an hour. If I know I don't have an hour, I ask for as long a period of prayer as I have time for. Sometimes that is half an hour. Other times it might be forty-five minutes.

Along with praying about the quantity of time, I also use this period of preliminaries to pray about the quality of my prayer time. I have a great tendency to get distracted when I pray. I also know that sometimes my attempts at prayer have seemed ineffective and even boring. I don't think quantity of prayer without quality of prayer gets the job done any better than quality of prayer without quantity. I pray about the quality of my prayer time. Since the ministry of the Holy Spirit is to help me to pray, I might pray something like this:

> Holy Spirit, help make this time of prayer pleasing to the Father. Make this time fruitful, real, focused, enjoyable, and experiential.

Remember, the Bible tells us that we do not have because we have not asked (James 4:2). Most of us have never thought about *praying* about our praying. This preliminary part of our prayer time sets the stage for what follows.

ABBA

Having appropriated the helping ministry of the Holy Spirit, I focus my thoughts on my relationship with God as my heavenly Father. I have developed a small notebook that I use as I work through my prayer time (Appendix A). Roman numeral one is entitled "Entering His Presence." I enter the Father's presence as I call out to Him, "*Abba.*"

Two powerful words in the New Testament teach us about our unique relationship with the living God. One of these words appears in both the Matthew and Luke texts where Jesus taught the disciples to pray. It is the Greek word *pater.* This word is appropriately translated *father.* The other is the word *abba,* the word with which Jesus addressed the Father in His prayer in the Garden of Gethsemane (Mark 14:36). *Abba* is actually an Aramaic word and a term of great endearment. It is probably best translated by our word *Daddy.* As a Christian, I now have the privilege of coming to God as both *pater,* Father, and *abba,* Daddy! The Bible tells us that the presence of the Holy Spirit in our lives is a spirit of adoption, which provides this privilege as a part of our spiritual birthright (Romans 8:16; Galatians 4:6).

I am the father of two tremendous kids! My daughter, Stephanie, is ten as I write this book, and my son, Baker, is four. I will always be their father, and I hope they will always know they have the privilege and right to climb up in my lap and call me Daddy. The intimacy of our father-child relationship is a source of incredible, even indescribable, joy to me.

When my son was two and a half, he was having a hard time learning to talk. In the word of the experts, he was delayed. One Tuesday morning I was up very early to finish preparing to teach the men's Bible study. I was teaching on a passage in Ephesians 1 which tells us that, in Christ, God predestined us to be adopted as His children (v. 5). Baker woke up early and came out of his bedroom to find me sitting on the family room sofa going over my notes. He climbed up next to me on the couch and began to drink from the bottle we had left out for him. Suddenly, as if a light bulb went on in his mind, he looked up at me with a big smile, put his index finger on my arm, and declared, "Baker's daddy!" At that moment he could have asked me for anything in the world, and I promise you I would have given it to him! I was thrilled by this simple recognition and affirmation. It was a tremendous illustration to me of how our heavenly Father delights in our coming to him as *Abba* . . . Father.

When we focus our attention on God as our Father, we consciously enter His presence. Theologically speaking, we are always in His presence, but prayer is first and foremost a time to spend time in His presence consciously and experientially. We enter His presence for a time of communion, fellowship, and relationship with our heavenly Daddy.

I have a confession that many people in my church will verify. I am often hard to get hold of and even harder to get an appointment with. My schedule is full to the point of being chaotic. Sometimes a person calls the church asking to set up an appointment with "Mr. Blitz." My immediate response to such a call is to assume this is probably someone trying to sell me something I don't need and can't afford. The probability of such a person getting an appointment is probably zero.

Another typical call might go something like this: "I'd like to see Reverend Beltz. I've never been to your church, but I know a guy whose aunt's cleaning lady once heard about someone who thought he might be interested in this new ministry I'm raising a million dollars for. Any chance we could get together?" Again, pretty slim odds for an appointment.

Some people get a little warmer: "Tell Dr. Beltz I'm a member of Cherry Hills. I've never been to one of his classes but I would like to get together to discuss sublapsarian Calvinistic antonomianism. Do you think he might have a few minutes?" Warmer, but probably still no appointment.

Now some folks get hot: "Tell Bob I'm a member of the Company of the Committed (the Wednesday evening group I teach). I need a few minutes of his time." This call probably gets an appointment as soon as I'm free.

But if the call sounds like this—"Daddy, can I talk to you?"—guess how I respond? You see, there are two little people on the planet that I will generally drop everything to talk to. They are the two who call me Daddy.

Know this! You have a Daddy in heaven who is perfect, loving, totally involved, gentle, present, available, concerned, kind, wise, caring, and good. He delights in your desire to spend time with Him. In light of this truth, I pray Ephesians 1:17: "Father, give me a spirit of wisdom and revelation that I might know You better." I pray that I will live in a relationship of heartfelt intimacy with the Father. I pray that the truth of the spirit of adoption will become real in my daily experience. I pray that this day I will live and walk in a father-child relationship with God. I pray that I will experience the truth that the Father loves me (*phileo*— heartfelt, emotional love) as He loves Jesus (John 16:27). I have come to believe that this relationship, affirmed and experienced, is critical to a healthy and vital prayer life. Slowly but surely, as I have prayed through this component in my prayer time, I have sensed the healing touch of God on my life. His fatherhood is becoming more experientially real in my life. The Holy Spirit is using the vehicle of prayer to bridge the gap between what I know in my head and what I experience in my life. I believe you will find the same expe-

---

"Know this! You have a Daddy in heaven who is perfect, loving, totally involved, gentle, present, available, concerned, kind, wise, caring, and good. He delights in your desire to spend time with Him."

---

rience beginning to happen in your own life if you spend adequate time praying through this first component.

During this preliminary time, I also pray that I might know and experience the lordship, friendship, and brotherhood of Jesus Christ. I pray that the Holy Spirit will fill my life and work in me as I pray. With my preliminaries complete, I am ready to move on to the second component of my prayer time: praise and worship.

ASSIGNMENT: WEEK TWO

1. Read Ephesians 1:1–14; Romans 8:12–17; Galatians 4:1–7.

2. Ask the Holy Spirit to help you pray ten minutes a day, five days this week.

3. Using your outline from last week, start to develop your prayer notebook (Appendix B).

4. Pray through the first component of prayer:
   a. Focus on your relationship with God as Father.

b. Pray through your father-child relationship.

c. Ask for the spirit of adoption to become real in your experience.

d. Pray about
  • walking with the Father,
  • the lordship of Jesus,
  • friendship with Jesus,
  • the Holy Spirit filling and controlling your life today.

5. Using the outline developed after chapter 1, pray briefly through the other components of the pattern.

WEEK THREE:

SEEKING HIS FACE

Four

"HALLOWED BE YOUR NAME"

If you are following the assignments in this book, you are now in your third week of building a more effective prayer life. If you are reading through the book before working on the assignments, I recommend that you go back through the book a second time and follow the suggested schedule. In either case, I want to warn you about an inevitable phenomenon. If you signed the statement of intent at the end of chapter 1, you have resolved to have a more effective prayer life. Following that resolution, you have tried to pray a certain amount of time at least five days a week. Now, let me ask you a question. How are you doing?

WARNING: BEWARE OF DISCOURAGEMENT

My hunch is that some of you might be discouraged. Discouragement is a great hindrance to developing our prayer life. I'm convinced that a commitment to a life of prayer causes a definite tremor in the heavenly realms. Our commitment will be challenged by the evil one. Sometimes his challenge produces temporary defeat. Temporary defeat leads to discouragement. Fortunately, it is easy to overcome discouragement. If you are having a hard time, keep plugging away. Persistence will defeat discouragement. If you had a bad week last week, work at having a better one this week. As you begin to add component to component in prayer, your personal strategy will become more exciting. The satisfaction of successful days will eventually overcome the discouragement. Hang in there!

PRAISE AND WORSHIP

By praying through the first component of our prayer strategy, we enter into the presence of the living God, who is now our Father. The second component in my time of prayer is a focused time of praise and worship. Jesus taught the disciples that they were to pray, "Hallowed be Your name." We have already observed that prayer is primarily a time of communication and fellowship with God. It is appropriate that we use part of our time to contemplate the majesty of God and to engage in the process the Bible calls "seeking the face of God." I believe this was Jesus' intent as He instructed the disciples to "hallow" the "name" of the Father.

In the culture of Jesus' day, a name carried great significance. A person's name was a reflection of character. Often when God had a powerful encounter with an individual, He changed the person's name to reflect the change in character produced by the encounter. The name of God is also a revelation of the nature and character of God. To *hallow* means "to treat with great reverence." We hallow the name of God as we worship His nature—who He is. Focusing our thoughts on who He is will lead us into praise and thanksgiving.

As I began to develop this dimension of my own prayer time, I had several important insights. I was immediately aware of how little of my previous ineffective prayer life was focused on God. Most of my prayer time was devoted to telling God what I needed and asking Him to do things. I was neglecting a critically important dimension of prayer. I needed to focus on God and who He is to even know how to pray about my needs. In the words of Jesus, I needed to "seek *first* his kingdom and his righteousness" (Matthew 6:33, emphasis added) to get my spirit in tune with the Holy Spirit.

To accomplish this objective, I followed some simple suggestions regarding how to use the actual name of God in prayer.

The Name of God

What is the name of God? The word *God* is not a name; it is a title. We use the title as a name, but it really isn't. In the

> *"Most of my prayer time was devoted to telling God what I needed and asking Him to do things. I was neglecting a critically important dimension of prayer. I needed to focus on God and who He is to even know how to pray about my needs."*

Bible, God has made His name known and then has repeatedly amplified on that revelation.

The book of Exodus contains the story of Moses. In the third chapter, we read how God called Moses to go back to

Egypt to lead the nation of Israel out of bondage. Moses responded to that call by asking God an important question: "Who shall I say sent me?" Moses was asking God to tell him His name. The living God answered Moses' question. God said, "Tell them I AM has sent you" In the Hebrew manuscripts, God's name is written with four Hebrew consonants. What we translate as I AM can be transliterated out of the Hebrew as *YHWH*. I have a book in my library entitled *YHWH Is Not a Radio Station in Minneapolis*. How true! *YHWH* is the proper name of the living God. If we add vowels to the consonants, we might pronounce the word as *Yahweh*. Later in biblical history, the vowels from the Hebrew word *adonai*, which means "Lord," were added to these consonants; and the word *Jehovah* was developed to express the name of God.

What does this name tell us about the nature of God? *YHWH* is a form of the Hebrew verb *to be*. It can be translated as *I AM* or in a causative sense as *I cause to be*. I like to think about the name in both of these ways. God is the God who *is* and who *causes to be*. I begin my time of worship in prayer by praising Him and thanking Him for this truth and by inviting Him to *be* and *cause to be* in my life this day.

The Names of God

As we move through the Old Testament from the Exodus 3 revelation of the name of God, we find that God revealed more of His nature by compounding the name *YHWH*. Each compound name reveals more of the nature of God. These compound names provide a great resource for our time of praise and worship.

In my prayer notebook, I have a section entitled "Seeking His Face." Eight of the compound names of God form the points of this section. I pray through each of these names as a guide to this component of prayer (Appendix A, II, p. 173).

YHWH-tsidkenu (Jeremiah 23:6). Two of these names relate to God's redemptive activity in human history. *YHWH-tsidkenu* means "the Lord our Righteousness." This is one of the names of God that reminds us of God's gift of salvation in Christ. Usually, at this point in prayer, I remember that Jesus' name in Hebrew was *Ya'shua,* which means "God is Salvation." I thank and praise God that, when I had no righteousness of my own and was in a desperate situation of need, Jesus Christ died and rose for me. He is now the source of my righteousness. Jesus fulfills the name *YHWH-tsidkenu* (1 Corinthians 1:30). I usually pause and reflect on what Christ has done for me. His atoning death and resurrection are the bases on which all of life takes on meaning and significance. I worship God for this gift.

YHWH-m'kaddesh (Exodus 31:13; Leviticus 20:7–8). Not only is the Lord my Righteousness, He is also the Lord who sanctifies. He not only declares me righteous in His eyes because of Jesus, He is also at work in my life to change me and make me righteous in my character and experience. Reflecting on this name of God reminds me of how desperately I need Christ to work in my life each day. I am eternally grateful for His gift of forgiveness. I have great confidence that the death of Christ was fully adequate to pay the price for the forgiveness of my sin. My forgiveness and God's declaration of my righteousness in His sight are finished business.

In my experience, however, I have light-years to go. I need to be changed. I am painfully aware that I am powerless over the results of my separation from God. Apart from His intervention, my life is unmanageable and unfruitful. Gratefully, as I think about the significance of God's name being *YHWH-m'kaddesh,* I acknowledge that He is at work in me to restore sanity and fruitfulness. That is why I praise and thank God that He is *YHWH-m'kaddesh.*

YHWH-shamma (Ezekiel 48:35). Immediately, I am reminded that the agent who makes my sanctification possible is the Holy Spirit. All that the Father purposed and the Son provided is made real in my experience by the ministry of the Spirit. By the ministry of the Holy Spirit, God is the Lord who is present. This name of God reminds me that my life has been invaded.

The most sacred piece of real estate in the land of Israel was the piece of turf on top of Mount Zion. That is where the temple of the Lord was located. The real importance of the temple was not to be found in what people did there. The unique characteristic of the temple was found in the fact that the living God had chosen to manifest His presence there. Although the infinite, living God cannot be contained in a building made by human hands, in love He decided to give His people a tangible manifestation of Himself in the Holy of Holies. There, between the cherubim and over the ark of the covenant, God was present in a unique way.

God no longer manifests His glory in a building made of stone. His great desire since the dawn of creation has been to manifest His glory in the lives of men and women. Because of the indwelling presence of the Holy Spirit, our bodies now have become the temple of the living God (1 Corinthians 3:16; 6:19). Jesus is our Immanuel—God *with* us. He is present. I praise Him and thank Him that He is present by the Holy Spirit and ask the Spirit to fill my life with that presence. God promises that He is with me always (Matthew 28:20) and will never leave or forsake me (Hebrews 13:5). He is *with* me and He is *in* me because He is *YHWH-shamma*.

Through the Gate and into the Court

The praise and worship dimension of my prayer time has become an incredible source of joy. I now know that this part, missing from my previous prayer life, is critical to a joyful experience of prayer. Psalm 100 instructs us to "Enter his gates with thanksgiving and his courts with praise" (v. 4). As we spend time in prayer focusing on the nature of God, we will begin to sense that we are in His presence. Prayer begins to be exciting and joyful because "in Your presence is fullness of joy" (Psalm 16:11, NKJV).

During the early days of praying through this component, I had another helpful insight. I used to wonder how to fulfill the exhortations of Scripture to seek the face of God (Psalm 27:8). After all, if God is Spirit (John 4:24), as He is,

> **"As we spend time in prayer focusing on the nature of God, we will begin to sense that we are in His presence. Prayer begins to be exciting and joyful because 'in Your presence is fullness of joy' (Psalm 16:11 NKJV)."**

what does His face look like? I began to see that the concept of the face of God also refers to the nature and character of God. In a sense, all of the attributes and names of God reveal different dimensions of His face. Seeking His face is seeking to know Him in all His wonderful fullness. As I was praying through the names of God and reflecting on what they meant to me, I was seeing the face of God. His face motivates praise and worship. In our church, we sing a song of praise in which we declare, "Isn't He beautiful!" Yes, He is. His face is beautiful.

YHWH-rohi (Psalm 23:1). Classics are usually classics because they are so . . . well, classic! That is certainly true of the twenty-third psalm. How many of us have read, memo-

rized, quoted, and reflected on this psalm without ever real-
izing that the opening declaration of David is one of the
names of God. *YHWH-rohi*, the Lord is my Shepherd. I
praise and thank God that He is my Shepherd. A shepherd
guides his flock. God guides me. A shepherd provides for
his flock. God provides for me. A shepherd protects his
flock. God protects me. A shepherd is the source of security
for his flock. God is that for me.

As I pray through this name of God, I pause and give
thanks for each of these characteristics of a shepherd. I always
pray that this day God, my Father, will shepherd me by guid-
ing, providing for, and protecting me. He is my Shepherd. I'm
also reminded that Jesus is the Good Shepherd (John 10:11). I
praise and thank Him that He is *YHWH-rohi*.

YHWH-jireh (Genesis 22:14). The record of the patriarch
Abraham's life offers one of the great revelations of God's
nature. Having waited until the ripe old age of ninety-nine
to have a son who would fulfill God's promise, Abraham
must have found it incredible that God could actually want
him to sacrifice Isaac. I could never understand Abraham's
seemingly instant obedience to God's command here until
someone pointed out that by the time God called Abraham
to sacrifice Isaac, Isaac was probably a teenager. Maybe it
wasn't as tough as we think! As Abraham and Isaac
trooped up Mount Moriah, Isaac must have been a bit sus-
picious. He asked his dad the proper question: "The fire
and wood are here . . . but where is the lamb for the burnt
offering?" (Genesis 22:7). You know the story. God saw
Abraham's willingness to sacrifice his only son. We can assume that this was all God was really looking for. God provided a ram caught in a thicket by its horns for the sacrifice.
In response to this divine intervention and provision, Abraham named the place *YHWH-jireh*, the Lord will provide.
Our God is a provider. He meets our needs. His name re-

veals His nature. He promises His provision, and the promise finds its fulfillment in the work of Christ and His providential care over our lives. As Paul wrote to the Philippians, "My God will meet all your needs according to his glorious riches in Christ Jesus" (Philippians 4:19).

Not only is He our provider. He is a good provider. Every good and perfect gift comes from His hand (James 1:17). He is also a provider of good. "No good thing will he withhold from those who walk uprightly" (Psalm 84:11, NKJV). As I focus on this name of God, I give praise and thanksgiving for His provision and faithfulness in my life. I praise Him that He is *YHWH-jireh.*

YHWH-rophe (Exodus 15:26). The provision of healing is intimately linked to God's very nature. As the nation of Israel was coming out of bondage in Israel, God made a wonderful promise to them. They had crossed the Red Sea and traveled three days into the Desert of Shur. The people desperately needed water and could find none. They came to a place called Marah where there was water, but it was bitter, unfit for human consumption. God used Moses to perform a miracle of healing on those waters to make them "sweet," or healthy. This event revealed a new dimension of God's nature. He promised the nation that, if they lived in obedience (which they failed to do), He would keep them from being afflicted with the diseases of Egypt. Then He spoke His name: *YHWH-rophe,* "I am the Lord who heals you."

The subject of healing is complicated. I confess that I don't fully understand it. I have been blessed to have experienced repeated instances in the life of my family when God's healing nature has been expressed in response to prayer. In my prayer times, I give praise and thanksgiving for those works of healing. If I am in a situation where I or someone in my family needs a healing touch, I pray about it. I worship God because He is *YHWH-rophe.*

YHWH-nissi (Exodus 17:15). During a normal prayer time, at this point in my praise and worship, I usually feel I have entered another zone. As you focus on who God is, what His "name" is and what His face is like, your prayer time should really be coming alive! All that God is, as revealed in these YHWH names, naturally leads me to praise and thanksgiving that he is *YHWH-nissi,* the Lord my Banner.

This name of God is given to an altar that Moses built after Israel defeated the Amalekites during the time of their exodus (Exodus 17:15). The significance of the name is the recognition that God is the source of victory and success in our lives. Because He is the source of my salvation, sanctification, security, provision, protection, guidance, and healing, I no longer need to fear. He has broken the curse of the law and the sources that create my fear of failure. He has promised me hope and a bright future (Jeremiah 29:11). He has shown me how to live a life of godly prosperity and success (Joshua 1:8). My life will not be free of difficulty, but every difficulty will be an opportunity to experience His victory. As I pray, I thank Him that He is my Banner and that His banner over me is love. I praise Him and thank Him that He is *YHWH-nissi.*

As you pray through the names of God in your time of praise and worship, you will often find your mind flooded with thoughts about the particular dimension of God's nature you are focused on. Often, these thoughts and insights are part of an answer to a prayer you have already prayed. You asked the Holy Spirit to make your prayer time real and meaningful. Now, He is interacting with your mind and giving insights as you pray. Feel free to stop and reflect and meditate on these thoughts. Some days, it has taken me over an hour just to pray through these eight names of God.

YHWH-shalom (Judges 6:24). The final name I pray through is almost a summary name. *YHWH-shalom* means "the Lord is Peace." Most of us remember the story of Gideon because of his famous fleece experiment with God. What we often fail to remember is that Gideon had a powerful encounter with the angel of the Lord prior to his fleece episode. In response to this encounter (which many scholars believe was a Christophany, or Old Testament visitation of Christ), Gideon, grateful that he encountered God and lived, built an altar. He gave this altar the name *YHWH-shalom.*

Gideon was used in this instance to reveal a profound truth: the Lord is Peace. The Hebrew word *shalom* is a much more comprehensive word than our English word *peace.* It

---

"Worship is vital to an effective prayer life."

---

encompasses well-being, contentment, harmony, satisfaction, and wholeness. In the Old Testament, the *shalom* of God was intimately related to God's blessing. The great blessing of God given to the Levites in the book of Numbers demonstrates this relationship:

> The Lord bless you and keep you;
> the Lord make his face shine upon you,
>   and be gracious to you;
> the Lord turn his face toward you,
>   and give you peace *[shalom].*
>
> (Numbers 6:24–26)

The blessing of God brings the peace of God. If you are a Christian, Jesus Christ is the source of your peace (Ephesians 2:14). One dimension of the fruit of the Spirit is peace (Galatians 5:22). I give praise and thanksgiving in prayer for the peace of God in my life. My well-being and wholeness come from Him. I live under the covenant of His blessing, provision, salvation, sonship, healing, victory, and peace. I give praise and thanksgiving that He is *YHWH-shalom*.

Worship is vital to an effective prayer life. Something happens in our hearts as we spend this time focusing on who God is. The psalmist wrote, "Delight yourself in the LORD and he will give you the desires of your heart" (Psalm 37:4). When we hallow the name of God and seek His face, we are really delighting ourselves in the Lord. If you are faithful to spend adequate time in this early part of your prayer, you will find that prayer becomes vital and exciting. You will have consciously entered His gates with thanksgiving and His courts with praise.

Having moved into His presence and seen His face, you will be spiritually prepared to move into the next component of prayer. As we worship Him, He prepares our hearts to seek His intervention in our lives. We are now ready to place many crucial areas of our lives under His will and to seek the present realities of His kingdom.

ASSIGNMENT: WEEK THREE

1. Reaffirm your commitment to pray.

2. Ask the Holy Spirit to help you pray fifteen minutes, five days this week.

3. Develop your own "Seeking His Face" section in your prayer notebook (Appendix B). For example:
   • Jot down what each name of God means to you.
   • Jot down Bible verses that come to mind for each name.

4. Pray.

   a. Pray through your preliminaries (See Week Two).

b. Pray through the *YHWH* names of God with deliberate praise and thanksgiving.

c. Briefly pray through the rest of the outline developed from the Lord's Prayer.

WEEK FOUR:

UNDERSTANDING DIVINE INTERVENTION

Five

"THY KINGDOM COME"—PART 1

As we move into the next component of our prayer time, we enter an incredibly exciting dimension of prayer. Jesus taught the disciples that a portion of their prayer should be given to praying for the kingdom of the Father to come and the will of the Father to be done. His qualifying, or amplifying, phrase in relation to this topic was "on earth as it is in heaven." Part of the incredible dynamic of prayer lies in the fact that authentic prayer brings heavenly realities to bear on earthly situations.

THE KINGDOM OF GOD

When I began to analyze the significance of Jesus' instruction at this point in His prayer outline, I had a degree of difficulty coming up with an appropriate title to capture the instruction and intention of Christ. At first, I decided to call this section "Calling Forth the Kingdom." The more I reflected on that title, the more uncomfortable I became. I thought it sounded a little too arrogant and perhaps a bit theologically warped—though in one sense we do call forth the kingdom when we effectively exercise this component of our prayer life.

To appreciate and apply this component of prayer fully, we must have a proper understanding of the kingdom of God. This concept permeated Jesus' life and teaching. From the beginning of His ministry when He declared, "The kingdom of God is at hand. Repent . . ." (Mark 1:15, NKJV), until His ascension to the right hand of the Father, when the disciples asked, "Will You at this time restore the kingdom to Israel?" (Acts 1:6, NKJV), the gospel is about the kingdom.

In the New Testament, the Greek word we translate kingdom is *basileai*. This word is used in two different and extremely significant ways. When you and I think of the concept of kingdom we usually think of the realm of a king. For us Western thinkers, kingdom speaks of geography. Often, we might think that where there is no geographical land mass over which a king reigns, there is no kingdom. It appears that, even to many people in Israel during Jesus' time, the concept of the kingdom was primarily connected to a military Messiah who would overthrow the Roman oppressor and reestablish a political kingdom over the same geographical area King David once ruled.

But, in biblical times, the word *basileai* was often used without reference to a geographical realm. In these cases, the word emphasized the *reign*, or *dominion*, of a king without the necessity of a geographical realm. In this sense, the kingdom exists wherever the king reigns, whether over a chunk of nearly barren geography in the Middle East or in the heart of a man or woman in downtown Manhattan.

Jesus often used the word in this way when referring to the kingdom of God. He taught that "the kingdom of God is within you" (Luke 17:21). In this context, Christ exhorted the disciples to "seek first the kingdom of God and His righteousness" (Matthew 6:33, NKJV). He was not instructing them to go on a search for an elusive piece of real estate. He was encouraging them to seek the rule and reign of God in their hearts as their highest priority. When they sought and achieved this objective, they would experience the reality of the kingdom. Heavenly priorities would then dominate and dictate the agendas of their lives.

At this point, it is important to realize that there is a realm where God reigns. He ultimately reigns over the en-

---

"Men and women on planet Earth have been given an incredible opportunity. Through the gift of prayer, these men and women have been invited to appropriate unseen kingdom realities and bring them to bear on earthly situations."

---

tire created and uncreated universe. For the moment, there appears to be only one piece of real estate in the cosmos that is not operating under His reign. You guessed it—a small, insignificant planet in the western spiral arm of the Milky Way galaxy, populated by, among other organisms, a peculiar carbon-based life form called man. Following certain transactions in what is often referred to as primeval history, the dominion over this piece of turf was forfeited to a character who himself had rejected the reign of God somewhere before the dawn of time as we know it. You and I have the good(?) or bad(?) fortune of living on what C. S. Lewis called "the silent planet." One day, what Jesus Christ has already accomplished through His atoning death and triumphant resurrection will be fully consummated. On that day, "the kingdom of the world has become the kingdom of our Lord and of his Christ, and he will reign for ever and ever" (Revelation 11:15). Until that day comes, a small group of men and women on planet Earth have been given an incredible opportunity. Through the gift of prayer, these men and women have been invited to appropriate unseen kingdom realities and bring them to bear on earthly situations.

Rather than entitling this component of prayer "Calling Forth the Kingdom," I decided it was simpler to call it "Appropriating Divine Intervention." This is Jesus' invitation to us when He tells us that, when we pray, we should pray, "Thy kingdom come."

THEN AND NOW

Once we have some understanding of the reign versus realm emphasis of the kingdom concept, we also need to understand something of the timing dynamics of the kingdom, the eschatological dimension of this prayer concerning the coming of the kingdom. For years I believed that prayer for the kingdom to come was about the second coming of Christ and the fulfillment of Revelation 11:15. Certainly, that is one dimension of what Jesus was teaching. But we live in a unique period of history when it is possible to experience what George Ladd called "the presence of the future."

Through Jesus Christ, the kingdom of God has made a secret invasion of the planet Earth. In the Old Testament, the people of God understood history in a relatively simple, linear fashion. They knew that their age, or period of history, had been seriously warped by humanity's distorted relationship with God and the consequences of the Fall. They also knew that, in a future time of incredible upheaval, God was going to overthrow the current regime and establish His kingdom. This transition period was called the Day of the Lord (see Illustration 1). Following this period of upheaval, the kingdom of God would be firmly established in the Age to Come.

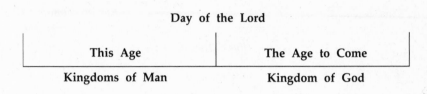

Illustration 1

With the incarnation of Christ, all that changed. At a pivotal point in His ministry, Jesus was casting demonic spirits out of human beings whose lives were under the controlling influence of the evil one. Rather than being ecstatically happy about these things, some of the members of the powerless religious establishment accused Him of actually casting out demons by the power of a character named Beelzebub, who apparently had been identified as one of the main movers among the demonic forces of Satan. Jesus' response was poignant. He said that, if Satan was casting out Satan, he would be destroying himself, which was a foolish and ignorant idea at best (Matthew 12:26). He went on to affirm that if, in fact, He was casting out demons by the power of the Holy Spirit (which He was), then the kingdom of God had come upon them (which it had) (Matthew 12:28). The future had arrived! Heavenly realities were being brought to bear on earthly situations. The kingdom had come, and there was a real presence of the future (see Illustration 2).

What does all of this kingdom theology have to do with your prayer life? Everything! There is an exciting present application of the prayer "Thy kingdom come."

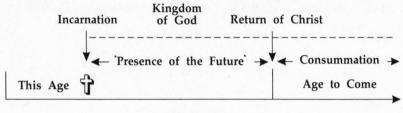

Illustration 2

THE KINGDOM AND YOUR PRAYER LIFE

We live in a time when the presence of the future is a con-stant possibility. We have the privilege and responsibility to pray that heavenly kingdom realities will intervene and in-fluence earthly affairs. Jesus told us to pray that the king-dom would *come* and the will of God would *be done* on earth as it is in heaven. In the Greek text, the verbs in these instructions are in the aorist tense and imperative mood. The degree of urgency and entreaty borders on authority and command in this grammatical structure. There is a nowness to these requests. When we pray this prayer, we are calling upon God to intervene in our lives and in our world.

It is important to notice several characteristics of this plea, or entreaty for divine intervention. Remember that we come to this point in our time of prayer only after a period of extended worship in which our hearts and minds have been set on God Himself. I have come to believe that this period of focus on God is essential to prepare us to pray properly for His intervention.

Notice also that, even as we shift from praise and wor-ship into the initial stages of what we might call interces-sion, we are still to be on God's agenda. Our intercession is to be about *His* kingdom and *His* will. In a sense, this com-ponent of prayer begins in a spirit of relinquishment. We

are saying to the Father, "Not my will but Thine be done
. . . not my kingdom first, but Your kingdom first!" This
spirit of relinquishment is then followed by an authoritative
entreaty. When we pray for the realities of the kingdom to

**"We have the privilege and
responsibility to pray that heavenly
kingdom realities will intervene and
influence earthly affairs."**

---

come to bear on earthly situations, we should expect that
they will. Jesus instructed the disciples to pray this way
with the expectation that their prayers would effectively release His power on earth.

Let me illustrate. In the twelfth chapter of Acts, we learn
that Peter was arrested and thrown in prison. Considering
that Herod had just put James, the brother of John, to death,
we can assume that Peter was in serious trouble. What was
the response of the church to Peter's predicament? We are
told that "the church was earnestly praying to God for him"
(Acts 12:5). What do you think that they were praying for?
Personally, I don't believe they were asking God to help
Peter accept his circumstances. I don't even think they were
praying that Peter would be comforted in his hour of need.
I don't believe they were praying that Peter would accept
his seeming eminent departure from the planet. I believe
they were praying for divine intervention—bringing the
power of heaven to bear on Peter's earthly circumstance!
We are also told how they were praying: "The church was
earnestly praying" for him! It appears that, with a degree of
appropriate authority, they were praying, "Come! Come,

kingdom of God, on Peter's imprisonment." They believed that perhaps it was *not* God's will for Peter to die yet, so with strong, earnest entreaty they were praying a command: "Will of God, be done!" The results were quite exciting.

Blatant divine intervention occurred. God answered the prayers of the church. He sent an angel, who woke up Peter (without waking up the guards he was chained to), released the chains that bound him (still without waking up the guards), and led Peter right out of the prison. They walked by the guards, who were apparently blinded, and out of the iron gate of the city (which opened all by itself). Peter was free! Heavenly realities were brought to bear on earthly circumstances in direct response to the prayers of God's people. This was not a Steven Spielberg special effect! This was real. The event was so powerful that not even Peter believed it was actually occurring. The text tells us that he thought he was having a vision (Acts 12:9).

In one of the more humorous passages in the New Testament, Peter went to the house of the men and women who were praying for him. They were still praying when Peter knocked at the door. When the servant girl reported that Peter was at the door, their response was classic. "You're out of your mind," they told her (Acts 12:15). The church didn't have the faith to believe God would actually do what they had prayed about. I'm afraid that, too often, I can relate. Meanwhile, Peter was still knocking. Finally, they opened the door. The text says they were astonished. I believe that is one of those great biblical understatements. Maybe the light bulbs finally went on: "Wait a minute! Peter gets jailed; we pray; God springs him! God answers prayer!" His kingdom had come and His will had just been done. I have a feeling that the personal prayer life of everyone involved in that episode took on a whole new vitality.

Here is the point. Jesus has given those who bear His name the privilege of appropriating divine intervention in prayer. Don't get me wrong. This is not the old name-it-and-claim-it theology. We don't change the will of God. It is not *our* kingdom we pray for. We affirm the will of God through prayer and bring the reality of *His* kingdom to bear on our lives. What an exciting privilege! I hope you capture the incomprehensible opportunity that sits at your fingertips and awaits your appropriation and application.

With these facts firmly implanted in our minds, let's look at how we can apply this component of prayer to several of the most strategic areas of our lives.

ASSIGNMENT:

The assignment for week four will appear at the end of the next chapter.

APPROPRIATING DIVINE INTERVENTION:
Part 1

Six

"THY KINGDOM COME"—PART 2

O nce we understand the presence of the kingdom of God in this age and begin to believe that Jesus has invited us to appropriate divine intervention, we need to develop a strategy for using this privilege. In each of our lives in many ways, we desperately need the touch of God. Adapting Dr. Larry Lea's pattern to my own life, I always try to pray through five general areas in which I daily desire to see God intervene and in which I believe He desires to see His will accomplished.

AREA ONE: MY LIFE

Jesus Christ has given us permission to seek divine intervention in our lives. I take advantage of that permission by using this time to pray for my own personal spiritual needs.

I begin this component of prayer by affirming that I desire that the kingdom would come in my life and the will of God would be done in my life. This is both a prayer of relinquishment and a prayer of appropriation. Then I pray through many specific dimensions of my relationship with Christ and what I believe He desires to accomplish in my life.

Early in my pilgrimage to build a more effective prayer life, I had a meaningful experience with the Lord. I was working on developing this section in my prayer notebook when I sensed that the Holy Spirit was communicating with me. I was wondering what would be appropriate items to pray about for my own life. As I thought about this issue, a question floated into my mind. The question was "What do you want?" The question was followed by the Scripture reference James 4:2. I knew the reference. It is the statement that often the reason we do not have something is simply that we have not asked God for it. That statement is followed by another that reminds us that sometimes we ask for something and don't receive it because our motivation is improper. I began to realize that many things I would like to see God do in my life flow from proper motivation and are fully consistent with God's revealed will. I began to make a list that has become a tool for praying about my own personal spiritual needs. My list includes the following:

1. Relinquishment to the will of God

2. Affirmation of my powerlessness

3. Request to be filled with the Spirit

4. Abide in Christ

5. Be pleasing to the Father

6. See His face

7. Hear His voice

8. Know His will

9. Remove the defects of my character

10. Spiritual maturity and stature

11. Character that He can prosper and empower without corruption

12. Gently create biblical humility

13. Fruitfulness in ministry

14. Walk in the new person

15. Obey willingly and joyfully

16. Blessing

17. Protection

18. Availability

These are only some of the areas where I ask for God's intervention in response to the question "What do you want?" Having prayed about my own spiritual needs, I move on to pray for divine intervention for my family.

"I began to realize that many things I would like to see God do in my life flow from proper motivation and are fully consistent with God's revealed will. I began to make a list that has become a tool for praying about my own personal spiritual needs."

AREA TWO: MY FAMILY

I believe God has given me no greater privilege and responsibility as the biblical head of my family than to pray for my wife and children. I believe that I have a double measure of authority as I pray for them. I have the authority

God has given me as a husband and father as well as the authority Jesus has given me to pray for His kingdom and will. Not taking advantage of this authority violates my responsibility and neglects my privilege. I wonder how different our world would look if more moms and dads were faithful to pray for their marriages and families? Certainly, families today are constantly pressured by the forces of this world pressing in on them. Also, I believe powerful forces of evil are at work, undermining God's foundational institutions like the family. How desperately our families need the intervention of the power of the kingdom of God!

Recently, a doctor friend of mine was flying back to Denver with his wife. A young woman was sitting in the window seat next to his wife. When the stewardess brought their meals, the young woman declined, stating rather pridefully and arrogantly that she was fasting. After the stewardess left, my friend's wife turned to the young woman and asked if she was fasting because she was a Christian. The young woman laughed in her face. She informed my friends that not only was she *not* a Christian, but that, in fact, she was a satanist. She told my friend's wife that she and her coven were fasting and praying to Satan for the destruction of Christian marriages. She then added, "Especially the marriages of Christian ministers!"

I had several reactions to this story. First, a cold chill ran down my back. Then, I was angry that such things could be true in modern America. Third came a kind of conviction, and embarrassment, that someone who followed and actually worshiped the evil one took prayer more seriously than I often did.

The Bible clearly teaches that our struggles in life are often not a matter of flesh and blood, but rather of principalities and powers (Ephesians 6:12). The real issues and battles are being decided in the heavenly realms. The vitality and welfare of my marriage and family are being influenced by unseen realities that are only influenced by fervent, effective prayer. How glad I am that Christ woke me up and began to help me pray "Thy kingdom come" in the life of my family.

When I pray for Allison and the children, I pray specifically for each of them by name. I pray something like:

> Father, I pray Your kingdom would come on Allison today. Holy Spirit, bring the realities of heaven to bear on her life today. Bless her, prosper her, and protect her. Father, Your will be done in Allison's life today.

Then, I pray for the specific needs Allison is facing. I pray that she would be happy; I pray that she would experience kingdom worth, that her sense of esteem would come from her walk with Christ. I pray she would have good friends and people to help her with her tasks. I pray that she would be the queen of our house and that God would

---

"The vitality and welfare of my marriage and family are being influenced by unseen realities that are only influenced by fervent, effective prayer."

---

be glorified in our marriage. Once, as I was reading Isaiah 61:3, I sensed that I should pray this verse of Scripture on Allison's behalf. Now I pray that God would bless her with "the crown of beauty, the oil of gladness, and a garment of praise." I'm not sure what God wants to do in her life, but I do know that she is a beautiful, happy woman who loves to worship the living God!

Our prayer for a marriage partner can be as expansive as our creativity. We all need so much divine intervention in so many areas of our lives that if God has blessed us with a believing life-mate, we need desperately to be praying for one another. I am convinced that the power and presence of prayer in our marriages can help us make it through the tough times that we all have. As we pray for our mate, God will show us our own need to change attitudes and actions to foster the good we seek. If you want the kind of relationship that God intended you to have with your husband or wife, prayer will be a major factor in seeing that desire realized.

I love praying for my two children. Ali and I have been blessed with two of the greatest little people on the planet! I long for them to have the best quality of life possible. I want them to know and experience the kingdom of God in their lives and to know and live out the will of God. I pray individually for each of them as I do for Allison. Again, I might begin like this:

> Father, I pray for Stephanie today. I pray that Your kingdom would come on her life. I pray that, by the power and ministry of the Holy Spirit, You would bring heavenly realities to bear on her today. I pray that Your will would be done in her life today.

I then pray that God would bless Stephanie and protect her. I pray that His plans and purposes would be worked out in her life. According to Luke 2:52, I pray that she would grow in wisdom (intellectually) and stature (physically) and in favor with God (spiritually) and people (socially). I pray that she would be a kingdom kid this day.

Several years ago, Allison and I were going through an especially difficult time. Our son, Baker, was a year old and having serious physical problems. Generally he was a real sick little puppy! The specialists at Children's Hospital had put him through every test imaginable to try to discover the source of his problems. As I was praying and searching the Scriptures, I came across a great passage in Psalm 144, and the Holy Spirit "zapped" me. I came to the conviction that God was giving me a promise for both of my children. Verse 12 of that psalm states:

> Then our sons in their youth
>   will be like well-nurtured plants,
> and our daughters will be like pillars
>   carved to adorn a palace.

I use this passage when I pray for my children. I began to pray that God would make Baker like a well-nurtured plant—healthy, vital, strong, and growing—a plant that *thrives*. Stephanie, at age 7, already looked like a pillar carved to adorn a palace. I began to pray that God would give her inner purity to match her outer beauty. I pray that she would not be defiled by her friends, future boyfriends, future husband, or by us as we, with all of our flaws, raise her. I pray that she will grow up to be a woman of God.

As I write, Baker is four years old. He is our little miracle boy. When the prognosis for him was bleak, hundreds of people in our church began to pray faithfully for him. Ali and I had prayed for him, had him prayed for by people with faith in healing, had hands laid on him, and even had him anointed with oil. God didn't choose to use any of those vehicles to bring healing. I had never shared with our whole congregation how sick Baker was. With a difficult Thanksgiving at Children's Hospital ahead of us, I shared our struggle from the pulpit on the second Sunday of November. The outpouring of prayer began that day. Two weeks later, when Baker entered Children's Hospital again, three days of intensive testing showed a marked improvement. He began to *thrive*. He began to change into a well-nurtured little plant. That was over three years ago. I am convinced that God wanted to use the prayers of the Body to release His healing power in Baker's life.

For Baker, I pray many of the same things I pray for Stephanie. Because of his unique needs, I also pray daily for his health, nurture, strength, and peace. The circumstances of his life have been so unique that Allison and I are convinced God has a special call on his life, so I pray that he will grow up to be a diplomat for the kingdom of God.

The final act of my day in relation to Stephanie and Baker is to pray for them. Since the day they were born, I have followed the same practice every night that I am home. After our final good-night conversations and a few shared songs of worship, I lay my hands on them and pray for each of them, closing with the Levitical blessing of Numbers 6:

> The Lord bless you and keep you;
> the Lord make his face shine upon you
>   and be gracious to you;
> the Lord turn his face toward you
>   and give you peace. (vv. 24–26)

When I have prayed faithfully and consistently for my children, I have a great sense of peace about their lives. Allison and I pray for them as if we are building a spiritual fortress around them. Our little ones are growing up in a crazy world. The battle is raging in the heavenly realms. As Christian moms and dads, we have a tremendous privilege and a staggering responsibility to pray for our children. We have been vested with a unique spiritual authority over their lives, and we must discipline our prayer time to use it.

At this point in my prayer time, I have prayed about two of the most significant priorities in my life. As you begin to put these ideas into practice, you might discover how little time you have been giving to this incredibly important work of prayer. Having prayed for divine intervention for my own life and the lives of those in my family, I want to make other uses of my privilege to pray, "Thy kingdom come . . . Thy will be done." We'll look at those areas in the next chapter.

"When I have prayed faithfully and consistently for my children, I have a great sense of peace about their lives. Allison and I pray for them as if we are building a spiritual fortress around them."

ASSIGNMENT 1: WEEK FOUR

1. Entitle a new page in your prayer notebook "Divine Intervention" (Appendix B).

2. Ask the Holy Spirit to show you the dimensions of your own life in which you should seek divine intervention. Ask yourself, "What do I want God to do in my life? What are the spiritual needs and kingdom issues I need to be praying about in my life?" Write your list under capital A of your divine intervention page.

3. If you are married and have a family, do the above exercise for each member of your family. Add your lists to your prayer notebook.

4. Ask the Holy Spirit to help you pray twenty minutes, five days this week.

5. Pray; work through the first two components of relationship and worship. Add this third component of appropriating divine intervention for yourself and your family (if applicable).

6. Pray through the rest of the Lord's Prayer using the other components in your outline as a framework.

APPROPRIATING DIVINE INTERVENTION:
Part 2

Seven

"THY WILL BE DONE"

Having thoroughly prayed about your family's spiritual needs, you now can use this component of your prayer time to pray for God's intervention in the affairs of the world. Jesus taught the disciples that they should pray that God's will would be done on earth just as it is always done in heaven (Matthew 6:10).

We live in a time so chaotic and filled with so many difficulties that it is easy to forget that God is still at work in it. Not only is God at work; He has plans and purposes for our world that we cannot even comprehend. In His divine sovereignty, God has decided to use people to accomplish His purposes. Prayer is one vehicle through which we take part in what God is doing and wants to do in our world. I begin my time of praying for the world by praying for the primary vehicle through which God has chosen to mediate the realities of His kingdom in this age.

AREA THREE: THE CHURCH

Over the last nine years, I have had a remarkable experience for which I am truly grateful. In early 1981, a small group of men and women had a growing sense that we were being led to plant a new church in South Denver. We couldn't have imagined what an exciting adventure was ahead of us. On March 7, 1982, the first worship service of Cherry Hills Community Church was held. Over the last eight and a half years, the kingdom of God has repeatedly come on the men and women who are part of this unique fellowship. By April of 1989, when I began to allow God to transform my prayer life, we had grown to an average Sunday attendance of four thousand, with another thousand children in Sunday School. I am convinced that much of the life of our church can be traced to the faithful remnant of men and women who have been committed to praying for the church.

I recognize that my being part of a vital, caring, dynamic, growing fellowship is not the experience of many church members across our country or around the world. But I also recognize that where excitement, vitality, and growth are, there are usually people praying.

When I began to understand the implications of Jesus' invitation to appropriate divine intervention through prayer, I could think of no greater need and opportunity than to pray for the church. I also recognized that I didn't have an effective strategy for praying for the church. I once again asked the Holy Spirit to help me pray. A familiar thought drifted into my mind. The thought was "What do you want?"

At first glance that seems like a rather foolish question. As a matter of fact, it seems almost as foolish as Jesus asking the man by the pool of Bethesda if he wanted to get well (John 5:6). The intention of both questions is the same. The questions suggest that sometimes we don't want to be healed personally and that we may not really want the church to be all that God wants it to be. Over the years, I have watched church people repeatedly develop levels of comfort that they don't want changed. If you are comfortable with the status quo, don't pray that God's kingdom will come on your church. God is rarely the God of the status quo. He was always most comfortable manifesting His presence in a moving tent called the tabernacle. The cloud by day and the pillar of fire at night rarely stayed in one

---

"I am convinced that much of the life of our church can be traced to the faithful remnant of men and women who have been committed to praying for the church."

---

place for very long (Exodus 13:21). Change accompanies life and growth. Tragically, whenever and wherever great revival occurs, the church itself often resists the changes revival brings.

What do you want? Are you unwilling to settle for spiritual mediocrity, either personally or corporately? Do you long to see spiritual renewal and spiritual revival? Are you open to the possibility that God longs to see a new reformation? If so, then begin to pray that God's kingdom will come on your church and that God's will would be done in your church. Then stand back and see how God intervenes!

The Leadership

What areas of church life do we need to pray about? First, I believe we need to pray that the kingdom of God will come on the leadership of our churches. In our church, that means praying for the staff who work full time in vocational ministry and the elders who are vested with spiritual oversight and direction. In your church, perhaps that will mean praying for a pastor or priest and a board of deacons.

Who are the spiritual leaders of your church? They are the ones you must pray for.

Nowhere is the reality of spiritual warfare more hideous than here. Though the evil one is no fool, most of his schemes are quite predictable. If he can effectively compromise the leadership, he can keep the church from being effective and vital. Sometimes, that takes the form of obvious temptations. How often have you heard of someone being wiped out of the ministry because of marital unfaithfulness? Men and women called and anointed for ministry are rendered ineffective, churches are thrown into chaos, and often the reputation of the bride of Christ is tainted.

Other times, the leadership is rendered ineffective through spiritual burnout. The demands placed upon most pastors in active and vital congregations are truly amazing. In a sense, the more effective a pastor is in bringing the truth of God to bear on people's lives, in the power of the Spirit, the *more* problems surface. In vital church ministry, people get in touch with their needs, creating greater demands on the staff. These men and women need the constant ministry of the Holy Spirit in their lives for refreshment and protection. We must also pray for the elders who govern the church to have clarity of vision to lead the church according to the Spirit and not simply after the will of human beings.

If you worship in a large church with a multiple staff, you might be discouraged about your inability to remember to pray for everyone. Usually, our response to that frustration is to shoot up one of those vague "Lord, bless the staff" prayers. In our church, we have forty full-time staff in various areas of ministry and support. I have asked our people to pick five staff members to pray for consistently. That way, all of the staff would have a group of people praying for them regularly. Pray that your leadership will experience the kingdom realities of blessing, protection, fruitfulness, effectiveness, and faithfulness. Remember to pray for their families also, for family is usually a prime target in spiritual warfare.

The Spiritual Health of the Body

After I have prayed for the leadership of the church, I turn my attention to the spiritual health of the body itself. I pray for spiritual renewal within our congregation. I pray that, as a church, we will be built up spiritually in maturity, commitment, vitality, and impact on our city. I simply ask the Holy Spirit to move in our midst and bring heavenly realities to bear on our church needs.

The Ministry

As I began to pray for the health of the church body, I also began to pray for the ministry of the church. True spiritual renewal in the church often leads to spiritual revival in ministry. In praying for the ministry of the church, I had an amazing experience.

We are a church of four thousand who have outgrown our second facility in our eight years of ministry. Often, life around Cherry Hills is so chaotic that I have tended to think we could experience only minimal growth, but when I asked the Holy Spirit to show me how to pray, I felt led to pray for the people in the area of town ministered to by our church. As I began to pray for spiritual revival in our area of Denver, two numbers floated into my head. Brace yourselves! The first number was one hundred thousand. I sensed that I was to begin to pray for one hundred thousand men, women, and children in South Denver that Cherry Hills Community Church was to reach for Christ in this decade. I have to admit that praying like this stretched my vision! But why not? Is not God the God who tells us that He is able to do exceedingly abundantly beyond all we ask or even imagine (Ephesians 3:20)? Does God desire to see revival in our cities? Absolutely! Are there one hundred thousand men, women, and children in South Denver who need Christ? There are ten times that number! Once again I was struck with the question "What do you want?" and the statement "You don't have because you have not asked" (James 4:2).

The second number that floated into my mind was fifty thousand. I sensed that I was to pray that, of the one hundred thousand reached, fifty thousand would become part of our fellowship. Talk about parking problems! I know that what I have just shared might seem like an ego trip or empire building. But that is not the spirit of what I am saying at all. I don't know whether these things will happen. I only know that they could happen if enough believers prayed. Every Sunday afternoon in the fall, seventy-five thousand men and women gather inside Bronco stadium for a "religious" experience that borders on worship. They are fanatics. They lift their hands, stand up, stomp their feet, sing cheers, and act out an amazing repertoire of behaviors. All this for a relatively stupid game played with the inflated skin of a pig (which, I confess, I happen to love). Why not have fifty thousand men and women gather each Sunday inside the house of God and get excited about eternally significant matters? That is the spirit in which I pray for my church.

How are you praying for your church? It is *your* church, you know. What do you want to see God do? Do you want spiritual renewal? Are you praying for the pastoral staff and lay leadership? Are you praying for the spiritual life of the congregation? Are you praying that your church will be a force for the kingdom of God in your community? Are you praying for the will of God to be done? Prayer is the catalyst that unleashes the power of the Spirit to move in and through the church.

If, in fact, we live in the end times, if this is, in fact, a decade of destiny, the church of Jesus Christ must become all that Christ intends it to be. The body of Christ needs the

---

"Prayer is the catalyst that unleashes the power of the Spirit to move in and through the church."

---

movement of the Spirit of God to create unity, purity, power, love, and worship. That movement will be intimately related to the faithful prayers of the saints. Do you want to be a part of something great for God? Then pray for the church.

AREA FOUR: OUR NATION

In 1990, I had the privilege of traveling with a team of men and women to teach in the Soviet Union. This trip was only my fourth outside of the United States. As you can imagine, 1990 was an exciting time for a visit to the Soviet Union. Our team spent a week in the Baltic republics of Latvia and Estonia before we moved on to Kiev and finally Moscow. At the end of our time, we flew out of Moscow on Lufthansa Airlines. As the plane lifted off the runway, most of the passengers began to cheer. I don't know why the others were cheering, but I felt everyone was grateful to be heading for the free world. I know I was.

From Germany we flew into Dallas, Texas. As we walked down the ramp toward customs, we came to a door. Over the door was one of the most beautiful signs I have ever seen. The sign said, "Welcome to the United States of

America." As I passed through the doorway, I got down on my hands and knees and kissed the ground. I thank God I am an American.

We are so blessed! We live in the greatest nation in the world. But we must also understand that we are living during a critical period of our nation's history. This is a time of great danger for the United States. Our country is in a period of tragic moral and ethical decline. This decline is primarily the result of the influence of a small minority of men and women who work harder to promote their value systems than we Christians do. Never has there been a more critical time to pray for our nation.

Until April 17, 1989, I had been negligent in praying for our nation. After April 17, I developed a page in my prayer notebook to pray for America. At the top of that page I wrote the text 2 Chronicles 7:14. This verse declares a promise to the nation of Israel when Solomon's temple was dedicated, a promise with profound application for God's covenant people today: "If my people, who are called by my name, will humble themselves and pray and seek my face and turn from their wicked ways, then I will hear from heaven and will forgive their sin and will heal their land."

Today, our nation faces one of two destinies: revival or destruction. Our land desperately needs mercy, forgiveness, and healing. Those who are called by the name of Christ must follow this formula. We first of all must repent and turn from our wicked ways. We must humble ourselves. We must seek the face of the living God. And we must pray for our nation.

I pray for three areas of need in our nation. I pray that the kingdom of God will come and the will of God will be done in the lives of the leadership of our country. Again, in the past, feeling overwhelmed with the scope of praying for those in office, I didn't. Now, I have set realistic expectations. I have pinpointed men to pray for at each level of

government. I pray consistently for one of our state senators, one of our United States senators, and daily for the
president.

I pray about the moral condition of our country and ask
God to be merciful and forgiving. I pray that God would
heal our land and bring spiritual revival on a national level.

**"This is a time of great danger
for the United States. Our country
is in a period of tragic moral
and ethical decline."**

I pray that renewal in the church and revival in the land
would produce authentic reformation in our culture.

I also pray about specific issues which our nation faces.
Again, rather than being overwhelmed by the impossibilit-
ies, I focus on the possibilities and pray for those issues
most on my heart and which God has brought to my attention. At the moment, the abortion issue and pornography
top my list.

AREA FIVE: THE WORLD

Finally, I apply my privilege of praying for divine intervention to the world. I know that, by now, you are experiencing one of two responses to the application of this component of prayer. Some of you might already be feeling
overwhelmed. We have covered an amazing amount of ter-
ritory, and we are only halfway through the Lord's Prayer.
But the overwhelmed response can change into the second
response, a recognition of how many critically important

areas we need to be praying about on a daily basis. I began to realize that I needed to be spending significant time in prayer just to cover the topics that are close to my heart. How can you do it? You might set the alarm a bit earlier in the morning to rise and do your prayer workout.

Mother Teresa is one of my heroes of the faith. In a recent interview, she referred to herself as "a pencil in the hand of God." She said, "He does the thinking. He does the writing." Isn't that what we all want to be? We want to be men and women whom God uses in significant ways to accomplish His plans and purposes. The interviewer went on to ask Mother Teresa a series of questions concerning her day:

Q. What did you do today?

A. Pray.

Q. When did you start?

A. Half-past four.

That's how to be "a pencil in the hand of God." We probably aren't going to start at half-past four. But we might remember Mother Teresa as we climb out of the sack to appropriate divine intervention for a world in desperate need.

We could pray for an infinite number of needs in the world. Again, rather than becoming overwhelmed, you can decide on a series of issues and people you will pray for. I focus on world hunger, world peace, and world evangelism.

In relationship to the latter, I would call your attention to the book of Acts. The simple truth is that the apostolic movement with its faithfulness, power, and effectiveness was filled, energized, and made effectual by the prayers of the saints.

We live in a time when Jesus' prophetic promise of His return in Matthew 24 has the potential to be accomplished.

Jesus told the disciples that the gospel would be preached in all the world and then the end would come (v. 14).

Almost every major mission agency in the world today has targeted the year 2000 as the date to accomplish this

> **"The simple truth is that the apostolic movement with its faithfulness, power, and effectiveness was filled, energized, and made effectual by the prayers of the saints."**

task. The two great needs of the hour are resources and prayer. Some of the most committed and gifted Christians on the globe are out in the field laboring to fulfill the Great Commission. They are engaged in a spiritual enterprise and constantly engaged in spiritual warfare, and the battles on the mission field are often won or lost in the prayer closets of the sending churches. You can't pray for every worker in the world. You might not even be able to pray for all the workers your church supports. But you can pick a handful and pray faithfully and consistently for them. Day by day, you can bring them before the throne of grace and pray that God's kingdom would come on them by the power of the Holy Spirit and that God's will would be done in their lives and in their work.

These, then, are the five areas in which I seek divine intervention: (1) in my life, (2) in my family, (3) in my church, (4) in my country, and (5) in my world.

Let me close this chapter with a little story that has been fun for me. As I added this component to my prayer time, I decided to pray for several countries in which I have special interest. One of the countries I prayed for beginning in April of 1989 was Germany. The day the Berlin Wall came down I had a funny thought. I wondered how many other folks had been praying for Germany. I'm sure many had prayed fervently for years for that wall to come down. I have to admit that I certainly don't understand exactly how prayer works. God chooses, at times, to do amazing things based on the prayers of a single man or woman. At other times, there appears to be some sort of a critical mass of prayer that needs to be reached before God acts. I was humorously wondering, what if God needed just one more praying person to reach that critical mass on the Wall when I started praying? Who knows? But this we do know. There are multitudes of Berlin Walls in the world today needing the prayers of God's people to help knock them down. We have this privilege: to appropriate divine intervention as we pray, "Thy kingdom come . . . thy will be done!" Let's begin to use this privilege faithfully.

ASSIGNMENT 2: WEEK FOUR

1. Add to your prayer notebook sections on (1) your church, (2) your country, (3) your world. Ask the question "What do I want?" Develop a list of the issues and people you want to pray about (Appendix B).

2. Ask the Holy Spirit to give you twenty minutes in prayer, five days this week.

3. Pray through the first three components of your prayer notebook, adding your requests for divine intervention.

4. Pray through the remaining components briefly, as outlined in chapter 2.

WEEK FIVE:

PRAYING FOR PROVISION

Eight

"GIVE US THIS DAY OUR DAILY BREAD"

J anuary 1, 1980, was a pivotal day in human history. This day marked the beginning of a new decade. Something about a new decade makes us feel as if history is about to unfold new and exciting possibilities. That was certainly true for my wife, Allison, and me. You see, January 1, 1980, was the day our first child, Stephanie, was born. I became a father on that day, and my life has never been the same since.

I remember holding Stephanie in my arms and wondering what this precious baby girl needed from her father. I also remember walking out of the hospital that day and for the first time worrying about the strangest thing: life insurance. Up until that day, I was mostly concerned about making it day by day and month to month. Allison and I had learned to live on very little and at times mostly on faith. But something happened the day I became a father. I became conscious of my responsibility to provide for my child. You see, by nature, fathers are "wired" to be providers.

THE PRINCIPLE OF PROVISION

What is true of earthly fathers is also true of our heavenly father. He is concerned about our provision. His care for our care is revealed in the fact that Jesus instructed the disciples that they were to pray, "Give us this day our daily bread."

Notice again the sequence Jesus taught the disciples. For many of us, prayer time has primarily been focused on bringing our needs before the Father. Jesus taught the disciples that the Father knows our needs already (Matthew 6:32). He also taught the disciples that preoccupation with our needs reveals a lack of trust in God as provider (vv. 25–32). Sequence becomes critical. Our primary focus in prayer is to be on God's kingdom and His righteousness (v. 33). Even in prayer, we need to focus on God and His kingdom, then come to the Father for our own needs. Having hallowed His name and sought His face, having appropriated His intervention and relinquished to His will, *now* the time comes to ask for our daily bread. He cares, and asking is appropriate, but people do not live on bread alone, but on every word that proceeds from the mouth of God (Deuteronomy 8:3).

A logical transition takes place at this point in the Lord's Prayer. The first phrases of the prayer, taken as topics, all point to God: "Hallowed be *Thy* name. . . . *Thy* kingdom come . . . *Thy* will be done (Matthew 6:9–10, KJV). Now the topics have to do with *us*. Give *us* this day . . . Forgive *us* . . . Lead *us* (vv. 11–13, emphasis added). When we have first sought the kingdom in simplicity, it is appropriate to seek God's provision for our lives. By the time you come to this point in your prayer time, you have already given praise and thanksgiving for God's providing nature. As you spent time in worship, using the names of God as a tool, you gave thanks that God is *YHWH-rohi*, the Lord my Shepherd. One dimension of God's shepherding role in our lives is to lead us to green pastures and quiet waters. The shepherd God is a provider God. He is the source of my provision. More specifically, you have given thanks that He is *YHWH-jireh*, the Lord who will provide.

The history of the nation of Israel demonstrates that the lesson of provision is one of the most important ones we learn in our spiritual pilgrimage. This truth was certainly demonstrated in the exodus of Israel from Egypt. It didn't take long for their provisions to run out. Moses and the people expected a relatively quick trip across the Sinai Peninsula and into the land of Canaan. Unfortunately for Israel, what should have been about a two-week journey ended up being a forty-year wandering. During those forty years, God provided supernaturally for the nation. Six days a week, when the dew dried off the ground, a thin flaky substance was left on the desert floor. God called it "the bread from heaven" (Exodus 16:4). When the people saw it, they asked, "What is it?" (v. 15). That question in Hebrew could be transliterated *Man hu?* Eventually they called the substance *man ha*, meaning roughly, "it is what it is."

God's instruction was clear: "Each one is to gather as much as he needs" (Exodus 16:16). No one was to gather a surplus. When anyone did, it rotted. This was to be a day-by-day experience of God's provision. God faithfully provided the manna for forty years.

After forty years in the wilderness, a new generation prepared to enter the Promised Land under the leadership of Joshua. Moses reminded this new generation of the provision of God and what it was intended to teach:

> Remember how the LORD your God led you all the way in the desert these forty years, to humble you and to test you. . . . He humbled you, causing you to hunger and then feeding you with manna, . . . to teach you that man

does not live on bread alone but on every word that comes from the mouth of the LORD. (Deuteronomy 8:2–3)

God was teaching Israel the lesson of provision. His covenant is a covenant of provision. Therefore, as His children, we are to look to Him to meet our needs. We are to ask Him to meet our needs. We have a need for daily bread, too. In Christ, we are given the invitation and the authority to come to our heavenly Father and entreat Him to "give us this day our daily bread."

I have friends who think it is inappropriate to ask God to provide for their needs. They view this as selfish. They have been taught that, in prayer, we should only relinquish to the will of God and be content with our circumstances. There is certainly a degree of truth in this approach. It also has the appearance of great humility and spirituality. The problem with the approach is that it is not biblical. The Bible instructs us to ask for what we need and to pray about every area of our life that produces anxiety. God delights in our dependence on Him as the source of our provision. Often, we do not have because we have not asked (James 4:2).

PRINCIPLES OF PROVISION

As we enter into this period of our prayer time and seek God's provision for our lives, it is important to understand certain principles that apply to receiving our daily bread. God's provision is one facet of our relationship with Him that is conditional. If we meet His conditions, we can have confidence that He will provide. If we fail to meet them, God might choose to teach us by withholding His provision.

The first principle of provision is nearly self-evident. To be assured of God's provision in our lives, we need to be in the proper relationship with God. The promise of provision is for those in a father-child relationship with the Father. We must be in Christ, having received Him as Lord and Savior, in order to be under the covenant of His provision.

Along with establishing our father-child relationship, it is important that we are in fellowship with Christ to receive His provision for our lives. By this point in our prayer time, we probably are experiencing real spiritual communion with Christ. That fellowship should also be reflected in our consistent reading and study of His Word. Prayer and Bible study must go hand in hand for us to have a balanced life

> **"The Bible instructs us to ask for what we need and to pray about every area of our life that produces anxiety. God delights in our dependence on Him as the source of our provision."**

of fellowship with Christ. Prayer and Bible study must also lead to a life of joyful, willful, disciplined obedience. If we are not in daily fellowship with the Lord, He might choose to withhold His provision as a loving discipline to force us to examine our relationship with Him.

A primary area of obedience that God seems to condition His provision on is our obedience in financial stewardship. Throughout Scripture, faithfulness and obedience in giving are intimately related to our own experience of God's provision. If our use of the resources God has already provided does not reflect our understanding and commitment to His ownership and lordship, God is in no way under compulsion to continue to provide for us. The message of the Bible is very clear on this point: "Give, and it will be given to you" (Luke 6:38).

One of my favorite—and most convicting—illustrations of this truth is found in the Old Testament book of Haggai. Haggai was a prophet sent by God to minister to the people of Israel after they had returned to Jerusalem from their seventy-year captivity in Babylon. God had allowed the defeat of the nation and their dispersion as a discipline for their continual idolatry and immorality during the years of the united kingdom. He also crushed their false confidence in their empty religiosity by letting the Babylonians destroy the Holy City of Jerusalem, including the temple. After seventy years, God began to draw the Israelites back to Jerusalem to rebuild the city, its walls, and, of course, the temple.

At the time of Haggai's ministry, the people had been back in the land for sixteen years. The primary reason for their return was to rebuild the temple. Yet, after sixteen years, they had not even started the work. The resources God had supplied for the temple had been used instead to construct their own homes. In what is surely an early example of blatant spiritual disobedience, the people apparently justified and rationalized their behavior by saying, "The time has not yet come" (Haggai 1:2). They were living a life of misplaced priorities and didn't even realize that they were suffering the consequences. God sent Haggai to the people with a simple message: "Consider your ways!" (vv. 5, 7).

Even after learning the hard lessons of the captivity, this generation of God's people was still not meeting the conditions necessary to receive God's provision. The results of their disobedience in the area of stewardship were profound:

> You have planted much,
>   but have harvested little.
> You eat, but never have enough.
> You drink, but never have your fill.

You put on clothes, but are not warm.
You earn wages, only to put them in a purse
with holes in it.

(Haggai 1:6)

God had smitten the means of provision because of their misplaced priorities. They were not meeting His conditions.

The book of Haggai is one of those few instances in the Old Testament where the people actually listened to a prophet and did what God instructed them to do. By the twenty-fourth day of the same month, the people had started to work on the house of the Lord (Haggai 1:14–15). Their obedience was richly rewarded. God spoke several messages to them. To simplify, He said, "I am with you" (1:13; 2:4); "I will bless you" (2:19), and I will *provide* for you (2:15–19).

Our failure to meet the conditions of God's provision in our lives will have the same effect. If we rob God (Malachi 3:8), we rob ourselves. If, on the other hand, we demonstrate our dependence and trust in God through faithful stewardship, we will be blessed (v. 10). My wife and I have talked to many couples who tell us they cannot afford to tithe—to give at least one-tenth of all income to the ministry and work of the church. We have learned over the last twenty years that we cannot afford *not* to tithe. We need to live within the sphere of God's kingdom provision. In order to guarantee that provision, we work diligently to meet the conditions of provision. Money can be either a source of blessing in our lives or a curse. The choice is really up to us. If you are not willing to meet God's conditions, there is no use in praying for His provision. But, if you are wise enough to believe that God is the source of every good and perfect gift, and if you will live in obedient fellowship with Him, then you have been given the authority and privilege to pray for your daily bread.

DAILY BREAD

How should you pray for your daily bread? I use this component of my prayer time to pray about two general personal concerns. First, I pray about the real *needs* of my day. I am almost embarrassed by God's great goodness to my family. Generally speaking, I need not ask for daily bread, but rather thank God that He has already provided it. I'm sure a day could come when, like George Mueller, my family and I might sit at an empty table and thank God that He is going to provide food for a meal. At present, I have a refrigerator well stocked with a week's worth of meals. Believe me, I am grateful for that reality. But, by nature, I am insecure and need to pray that God will continue to provide for my needs. I pray that we will continue to live in His kingdom provision for our lives.

As I pray for daily bread, I pray about the other needs of my day. If it is a day when I am preparing to teach or am actually teaching, I pray about my need for Him to provide me with good content and empowered presentation. If it is a day when I am going to be with my family, I pray that He will provide my need for quality time with Allison and my children. If it is a day when I am tired and burned out, I pray that He will provide some green pastures, some quiet waters, and that He will restore my soul. I simply ask myself the question, "What is my daily bread today?" Then I pray about the *need* of the hour. I have learned to be specific, persistent, and tenacious in praying about these needs, because I believe that is how the Bible teaches us to pray.

Second, I pray about anxieties. I have many desires and sources of concern that really don't fall under the category of need. Yet, in both the Gospels and the Epistles, we are instructed not to worry about our lives (Matthew 6:25–34; Philippians 4:6–7). The antidote for anxiety is prayer.

When I first started using this pattern of prayer, I made a list of all the sources of desire and anxiety in my life. If I wanted it or worried about it, I decided to begin to pray about it. Some of what I pray about does seem trivial in the big picture of life, but is not unimportant to a Father who

---

"The antidote for anxiety is prayer."

---

cares about the most minute details of our lives. Some of these issues have a certain immediacy. My wife and I are currently trying to sell our home. That process could be a source of great anxiety. Instead, as I consistently pray about it, I have peace. Other issues I pray about won't even become issues for years. I pray about my children's college education. I pray that God will make it possible for them to go to a great Christian college. Since my son is only four, it might seem silly to be praying now, but since I have been anxious about it, I pray about it. One day, Stephanie and Baker will leave for that scary country called "college," and on that day I will have the confidence that years of prayer have been invested in their college experience.

I pray cautiously. I am always reminded that Israel grew discontent with manna in the wilderness and asked for meat. Meat they got! But it was a disaster! The psalmist tells us that God gave them what they craved, but sent leanness into their souls (Psalm 106:15). I would rather not have what I want if it is not God's perfect will for me. So I pray for what I want but ask God *not* to give it to me if it would not be a blessing.

Having prayed through both my needs and my concerns, I almost always come to the end of this component of prayer with a great sense of peace. I have been with my heavenly Father who is *YHWH-jireh,* the Lord who provides. I have already sought *first* His kingdom and His righteousness in prayer. I have sought to meet the conditions of fellowship and obedience required for His kingdom provision. I have come with faith and expectation, setting before the Father my needs, desires, and concerns. I thank Him that He is the source of my security and my provision. With all these things behind, I am ready to move on to the next component of prayer.

ASSIGNMENT: WEEK FIVE

1. Develop section IV in your prayer notebook (Appendix A, p. 173 and Appendix B, p. 187).

2. List the needs of your life that you need God to meet.

3. List the desires of your life that you would like to see God give.

4. List the sources of concern in your life that produce anxiety.

5. Review the passages of Scripture referred to in this chapter.

6. Ask the Holy Spirit to give you twenty-five minutes of prayer, five days this week.

7. Using your notebook, pray through the first four components of prayer.

EXPERIENCING SPIRITUAL CLEANSING

Nine

"FORGIVE US OUR SINS"

I love being a Christian! It is the ultimate no-lose proposition. All my life I have been involved in organizations and institutions based on performance. On athletic teams my performance dictated my opportunity to participate. After my performance peaked, I lost the opportunity to move on to the next level of competition. My athletic value was based on my performance. I also have twenty-five years of formal education. I can safely say that I am now educated beyond my level of intelligence. Academic achievement is based on performance. As long as I performed well, I could advance academically, and I was rewarded with good grades and important-sounding degrees. Even in my work as a teaching pastor, my success or failure is based on my performance. If I teach well and people are helped, I am recognized as a good teacher. When my performance slips and I am boring or fail to communicate effectively, I am regarded as a mediocre or poor teacher. In almost every arena of life we are evaluated and rewarded on the basis of performance. The problem with this criterion is the incredible amount of pressure it puts on us. We all know that we are eventually bound to fail. That's why I'm glad I am a Christian.

Becoming a Christian is the one experience of my life that was not based on my performance. I became a Christian on the basis of my failure and Jesus Christ's performance. The church is the one organization in the world with our corporate failure as its criterion for membership. We come together because of our powerlessness and lack of performance. I have always believed that the ultimate motto of the church is "We're all bozos on this bus!" If you believe you are a Christian because of something you have done or some standard of self-righteousness you have achieved, then you do not understand the clear teaching of the Bible: "All have sinned [past-completed action] and fall short [present-ongoing reality] of the glory of God" (Romans 3:23). Becoming a Christian is an act of grace: God's grace—"By grace you have been saved" (Ephesians 2:8).

Grace is God's unmerited, undeserved, unearned favor. Grace is part of the nature of God. In grace, the Father sent the Son to die an atoning death for the forgiveness of sin and to make possible the gift of salvation. I am a moral, ethical, and spiritual failure. In either attitude or action, I have broken all of God's absolute imperatives in the Ten Commandments. If I had to perform to earn a relationship with the living God, I would be in big trouble. The good news (meaning of the Greek word translated "gospel") proclaims that I am not accepted on the basis of performance. I am accepted, once for all time, on the basis of God's grace and Christ's cross. That is why I love being a Christian.

There is, obviously, much more to being a Christian than our initial experience of receiving God's grace. When I received the gift of grace, a permanent transaction took place that will never change. In the account books of God, this permanent transaction was recorded. The biblical term for that transaction is the word *justify*, meaning "to declare righteous." In the instant that transaction occurred, the person of the Holy Spirit invaded my inner life. The Holy

Spirit brought life where there had been spiritual death. He regenerated my human spirit by His presence. With this newness of life, a process of transformation began. God began to work within me to change my character, that I might become more like Christ. This transforming process is

---

"I have always believed that the ultimate motto of the church is 'We're all bozos on this bus!' "

---

intimately related to my daily relationship with God, and my daily relationship with God is not like the once-for-all-time transaction of justification. My daily walk is related to my performance. When I fail, fellowship is impaired. Because of my tendency to fail, I need a means whereby my ongoing failure can be experientially brought under the once-for-all atonement of Christ. Just as I need daily bread, I need daily grace.

To facilitate the experience of daily grace, Jesus taught the disciples that a primary component of their prayer time was to be confession and forgiveness. In the Lord's Prayer, He instructed them, and us through them, to pray, "Forgive us our sins" (Luke 11:4).

THE REALITY OF SIN

Have you ever been in a worship service in which several groups of believers were met together and used the Lord's Prayer in the liturgy? Everyone is boldly praying aloud until you come to this line in the prayer. Suddenly, you can feel the anxiety begin to build. What are we going to pray?

Will it be "Forgive us our debts"? Or will it be "Forgive us our trespasses"? Or will it be "forgive us our sins"? Usually the prayer ends with some inaudible combination of all of the above.

You might wonder why there is all this confusion over something as simple as the Lord's Prayer. The answer is the recognition that in the Greek text two different words are used in the Matthew and Luke versions of the prayer. If you look closely at the two texts (Matthew 6, Luke 11), you will see that Jesus taught this prayer on two different occasions to two different groups. Matthew's version was part of the Sermon on the Mount. In this context, *disciples* probably referred to a rather large group of followers. In Luke's account, Jesus seems to be teaching only the Twelve. Since in both instances Jesus was probably speaking in Aramaic, while the narratives were recorded in Greek, it is hard to know whether Jesus Himself used different words or whether Matthew and Luke simply chose synonymous words to translate Jesus' teaching.

In Luke's account, the word translated *sin* is the Greek word *hamartia*, the most generic New Testament word to communicate the concept of moral, ethical, and spiritual failure. The literal meaning of the word is "to miss the mark." The mark, or biblical standard for the conduct of life, is the very nature of God Himself. When our lives fail to measure up to the holiness and perfection of God's character, we miss the mark—we sin. Sometimes our missing of the mark is an unintentional violation of some boundary God has established. Such violations without premeditated willfulness are often called trespasses. Other times, our violations of the boundaries involve a degree of knowledge and willfulness. In such cases, the harsher transgression is more appropriate. Often, we simply fail by not doing what ought to be done. We fall short of the standard. In all of these instances, we have a problem. We create what Francis

Schaeffer used to call "true moral guilt." By that term, Schaeffer distinguished between the emotional experience of guilt feelings—which may or may not be related to some moral, ethical, or spiritual failure—and true guilt, which is a product of the actual violation of God's standards. These actual violations might not be accompanied by any feelings of guilt at all. True moral guilt recognizes the truth that all of us

---

"True moral guilt recognizes the truth that all of us have missed the mark. . . . This recognition is critically important, painful as it might be, for a healthy daily fellowship with the living God; and this component of our prayer time forces us to get honest with God and with ourselves."

---

have missed the mark and are habitually falling short of God's standards (Romans 3:23). This recognition is critically important, painful as it might be, for a healthy daily fellowship with the living God; and this component of our prayer time forces us to get honest with God and with ourselves.

GUILT

Since every person on the planet has the problem of true moral guilt, every man and woman has the need for daily, experiential forgiveness. Every religious and philosophical system in the world attempts to define what people really need to deal with the problems and difficulties of existential angst. The modern gnostics, who worship at the shrine of education, tell us that what people really need is more information. The modern gurus of Eastern philosophy, in its many forms and manifestations, tell us we need to discover our innate deity and escape the world of material illusion by experiencing oneness with the great "mush" god ("god" being a convenient word used to mean everything). The modern pharisee assures us that we only need to keep the law, and the modern materialist declares that more of the right "stuff" will solve our problems. Every system has a solution, but they all still leave us with true moral guilt. True moral guilt alienates us from God, alienates us from each other, and ultimately even alienates us from ourselves. Everyone deals with this issue in one way or another.

Many people handle guilt by repressing or internalizing it. This solution will ultimately destroy you. Guilt is like a cancer that eats away at the human psyche. Others attempt reeducation as the solution. They might advocate that guilt is simply the product of faulty programming of the human superego. Some seek to atone for their guilt by becoming religious or working at humanitarian causes. Tragically, some men and women deal with guilt by punishing themselves with a multitude of forms of self-abuse, from the blatant chemical abuses of drugs and alcohol to much more complicated forms of self-hatred such as depression and low self-esteem.

The problem with all of these solutions is the same: *they don't work!* There is only one effective solution for true moral guilt. That solution is now available to us in prayer.

FORGIVENESS

The word used in the Matthew account of the Lord's Prayer is usually translated *debt*: "Forgive us our debts, as we forgive our debtors" (Matthew 6:12). The word translated *debt* here, the Greek word *opheilema*, is usually used literally "of one who owes money to another." In this instance, it is used metaphorically of a debt we owe in relationship to God. The most vivid biblical illustration of this concept is found in Colossians 2:13–14.

In this text, we are told that, through the cross of Christ, our "written charge" has been canceled. The idea of a written charge again suggests indebtedness. The same word is also used to speak of a list of charges drawn up against a criminal. Whenever a criminal was convicted of a crime in the Roman world, a list of charges—or certificate of debt detailing the crime and the punishment—was drawn up. In noncapital offenses, when the punishment had been executed or the debt repaid, a word was written across the certificate of debt, the Greek word *tetelesthai*, meaning "paid in full." The certificate with the "paid in full" on it was a person's receipt guaranteeing no further retribution. In capital offenses, the Romans nailed the certificate of debt or written charge to the top of the cross, so that all who passed by the hideous scene of the crucifixion would know what led to the execution. You might imagine that this approach was a powerful deterrent to crime! We are told that, when Jesus Christ was crucified as a common criminal, Pilate had a written charge drawn up and affixed to His cross. Remember, Pilate had found no guilt in Jesus. So what did the written charge say? "Above his head they placed the written charge against him: *This is Jesus, the King of the Jews*" (Matthew 27:37).

From a human perspective, that message is what people saw when they passed by the cross of Christ that day so long ago. But from God's perspective, something much more significant was going on. Paul tells us in Colossians 2:13–14 that what God reckoned to be nailed to the cross of Christ was *our* written charge. You might conceptualize your written charge as a document containing every failure to meet God's standards morally, ethically, or spiritually in attitude, action, or intent. This certificate is a history of all the sin, trespass, and transgression of your life—past, present, and future. In my case, that would be a long and ugly document. When Jesus Christ was nailed to the cross, from God's perspective that document was nailed to the cross with Him. You and I are the reason Jesus suffered such a brutal execution. He was paying the price to cancel our certificate of debt. Just before Jesus died, He cried out from the cross. Most translations read that His cry was "It is finished" (John 19:30). If you look in a Greek text, you will find that this cry was actually one Greek word. He cried out, *"Tetelesthai!"* "Paid in full" was Jesus' triumphant declaration from the cross! In that instant, God took our certificate of debt and canceled it. In a sense, He wrote *Tetelesthai* across our record of sin: "He forgave us *all* our sins, having canceled the written code, with its regulations . . . he took it away, nailing it to the cross (Colossians 2:13–14, emphasis added).

EXPERIENCING FORGIVENESS

When you receive Jesus Christ as your personal Savior, your sins are forgiven. Guilt is removed and your conscience is cleansed. If you have authentically repented and received Christ's forgiveness, any further guilt feelings are not a product of true moral guilt. When we do sin, we are called to confront our sin honestly. The Holy Spirit within us will convict us when we blow it. Our response is to agree with His conviction by confessing our sin. The Greek word for confession literally means "to say the same thing." When we confess and repent, we can instantly experience the forgiveness and spiritual cleansing Jesus provided for us by His atoning death. The promise of God is "If we confess our sins, he is faithful and just and will forgive us our sins and purify us from all unrighteousness" (1 John 1:9).

We can work through several stages in prayer to enable us both to receive and to dispense forgiveness. The twelve-

---

"If you have authentically repented and received Christ's forgiveness, any further guilt feelings are not a product of true moral guilt."

---

step program of Alcoholics Anonymous has some helpful suggestions for this component of our prayer time. Steps four through nine of the twelve steps provide a helpful tool.

Step Four: Getting Honest.

Confession is total honesty with God and ourselves. Step four states that we "have made a searching and fearless moral inventory of ourselves."

On a daily basis, we need to allow the Holy Spirit to show us areas of our lives that need to be brought to Christ in confession. In the Psalms, David prayed:

> Search me, O God, and know my heart;
>   test me and know my anxious thoughts.
> See if there is any offensive way in me,
>   and lead me in the way everlasting.
>   (Psalm 139:23–24)

David recognized his need for God's spiritual cleansing. Knowing the tendency of the human personality to be blind to its own shortcomings and sins, David also prayed:

> Who can discern his errors?
> Forgive my hidden faults.
> Keep your servant also from willful sins.
> (Psalm 19:12–13)

In my prayer notebook, I have made a list of the flaws in my character that seem to be ongoing sources of struggle in my life. I regularly and honestly confess these to the Father, thanking Him for His grace and the atoning work of Christ, which covers (literal meaning of *propitiation*—Greek *hilasterion*) my sins. I then ask the Holy Spirit to show me specific sins that I need to confess honestly.

Step Five: Confession

Having invited God to search me and make known anything needing confession, I then confess. Step five of the twelve steps states that we have "admitted to God, to ourselves and to another human being the exact nature of our wrongs."

Confession is cathartic. It is like breathing out carbon dioxide so that we can fill our lungs with fresh air. When Allison was pregnant with Stephanie and again with Baker, we went through Lamaze classes together. Allison learned breathing to help her control the pain of labor. During one stage of breathing, she was to follow a series of short, quick breaths with one long, lung-emptying expulsion of air. This breath was called a cleansing breath. That is what confession is like. It is God's provision for spiritual cleansing.

The twelve steps advocate confessing not only to God, but also to another human being. Roman Catholics have always confessed to a priest as the one through whom forgiveness is mediated. Those of us in the reformed tradition have grown up in a spiritual climate in which confession is directly addressed to God without an intermediary. We also recognize a theological principle called the priesthood of all believers (1 Peter 2:9). In response to James 5:16, we need to recognize the value of sharing our struggles and failures with a brother or sister (a person of the same sex as ourselves), who supports and encourages us on our spiritual journey. I meet with a small group of brothers on a regular basis for this very purpose.

Steps Six and Seven: Change

The good news about the "good news" is that its message of power changes our lives. Confession is not an end in itself. Confession clears the "crud" off the deck so that God can work to change our lives. I fully expect that, over time, God is going to work in my life to transform my character in the areas that cause me consistent struggle. For the changes to occur, I have to be willing. Perhaps you have heard the joke: How many psychiatrists does it take to change a light bulb? Answer: Only one, but the light bulb really has to want to change! Spiritual life is like that. Remember the formula from chapter 2?

—— WILL POWER = MY WILL + HIS POWER ——

Step six of the twelve steps states that we "are entirely ready to have God remove all these defects of character." We come back to the same old question: "What do you want?" Having faced the enemy and realized it is we ourselves, are we willing to let God change us? Step seven goes hand in hand with step six: "Humbly ask Him to remove our shortcomings."

Our time of confession is a time when we call upon the power of God to change the defects of our character and our life patterns that do not conform with His will. The twelve-step program is so effective in producing change because those who use it fully and honestly are usually men and women who have come face to face with some destructive addiction in their lives. The truth is that we are all addicts. By nature, we are addicted to sin. Only the power of God, released through our willingness, can overcome that addiction. As with other addictions, the battle is won or lost one day at a time. That is why daily confession is important.

Steps Eight and Nine: Restitution

In the Lord's Prayer, Jesus attaches another condition to our experience of forgiveness. Not only are we to confess our sins, but we are to be willing to forgive those who have sinned against us. Sometimes, our sin is very personal and involves only ourselves and God. At other times, our sin inflicts pain and damage on other people on the planet. Sometimes the sins of other people inflict pain and damage on us. When we are the object of another's sin, it is human nature to become bitter and harbor resentment. We nurse our anger until it brews and boils. We find ourselves wishing ill on the one who has offended us. Suddenly, our inner life is filled with negative emotion. Often, the damage our bitterness does to our sense of peace and well-being is more destructive than the original offense. Understanding the negative impact of negative emotions, Jesus taught the disciples to practice a discipline of forgiveness.

Having received grace, we are to dispense grace. Part of our prayer time needs to be focused on remembering those who have offended us and then making a conscious decision of the will to forgive them. At first, at the feeling level, we might still struggle with the one who has offended us, but as we consistently will to forgive, God is set free to diffuse and disperse the negative emotion.

When our sin has caused emotional, spiritual, or physical damage to another, we are called to make restitution.

Step eight states that we "made a list of all persons we had harmed, and became willing to make amends to them all."

Step nine puts step eight into action: "Made direct amends to such people wherever possible, except when to do so would injure them or others."

This component of our prayer time can be incredibly liberating. It is the reconstruction time for a life ill-lived. It brings into our experience not only the love and grace of God, but also His incredible transforming power. It provides us with the guidance, motivation, and enabling power to reconcile our relationships with God and with our fellow

---

"Understanding the negative impact of negative emotions, Jesus taught the disciples to practice a discipline of forgiveness."

---

beings. It enables us to live with the experience of inner cleansing and the peace of God, which accompanies such a spiritual state. Take this time seriously, and I promise you will enjoy the fruits of your prayer work!

ASSIGNMENT: WEEK SIX

1. Create a "Confession and Forgiveness" page in your prayer notebook (Appendix A, p. 173).

2. Read carefully Psalms 51 and 32.

3. Under "Confession," make a list of the ongoing character defects that give you the greatest problems: envy, lust, coveting, foul language, and so on.

4. Ask the Holy Spirit to make known (convict) to you specific sin that needs confession and repentance.

5. Under "Forgiveness," list those people who have sinned against you. Remember to include mothers, fathers, husbands, wives, sisters, and brothers. Make a decision to begin to forgive these offenses.

6. Ask the Holy Spirit to reveal to you any people to whom you need to make restitution and what that restitution needs to be.

7. Make restitution.

8. Ask the Holy Spirit to give you twenty-five minutes in prayer, five days this week.

9. Pray through your notebook, adding this section on confession and forgiveness.

DEVELOPING SPIRITUAL PROTECTION

Ten

"DELIVER US FROM EVIL"

O ne of my favorite times of the day is the first few minutes after I wake up in the morning. I love those mornings when I went to sleep at a reasonable hour and I wake up before anyone else in the family. My very favorite mornings are the ones when I wake up and realize that I don't have to rush off to some early morning meeting or appointment. I know I can spend some quiet time sitting on the sofa enjoying the beauty of a Colorado morning. Our living room faces the mountains, and five large windows frame a perfect panorama of the entire front range of the Rockies. As I tumble out of bed and slowly shuffle down the stairs, I usually have one thing on my mind: coffee! Those first few sips of coffee, relaxing on the sofa, and looking out at the mountains combine to make these early mornings so enjoyable.

Everything I have just told you probably seems pretty normal. Now I have to confess that part of my morning ritual may seem a bit strange. Part of what I enjoy about my first cup of coffee is the cup itself. Over the years my wife and I have collected an assortment of colorful and humorous coffee mugs. Some mornings, just looking at my coffee mug and getting a small chuckle out of it seems to start my day off on the right foot. For instance, one of our mugs has two cartoon bears facing each other and engaging in conversation. One of the bears has what appears to be a large red-and-white bull's-eye on his chest. The other bear, looking at the bull's-eye, comments, "Bummer of a birthmark!" I know it sounds strange, but somehow a cup of coffee out of that mug just seems like a great way to start the day.

One of our mugs is both humorous and profound. The mug has a series of wild animals dressed in suits, with briefcases, heading into a metropolitan scene complete with skyscrapers. The caption on this mug is written inside the cup so that it faces me when I take that first drink. In large capital letters this mug reminds its user, "IT IS A JUNGLE OUT THERE." This mug not only puts a smile on my face, but it elicits an affirming nod of the head and reminds me why I need to follow my morning cup of coffee with a hearty time of prayer. It *is* a jungle out there. Actually, it is much more dangerous than a jungle. A jungle is full of known and at times dangerous natural enemies. Our world is filled with unknown and dangerous supernatural enemies. We need a coffee mug that reminds us daily that it is a *war zone* out there. Our mug needs to be inscribed with the reminder the Apostle Paul gives in Ephesians 6: "For our struggle is not against flesh and blood, but against the rulers, against the authorities, against the powers of this dark world and against the spiritual forces of evil in the heavenly realms" (v. 12). You and I live in a supernatural universe. In this supernatural universe, you and I are engaged in spiritual warfare. We are intended to be spiritual warriors.

I remember living through the turmoil of the Vietnam War. I was a high school and college student during those years and never actually fought in the war. But I was right in the middle of the debate about the war back home. During those years, there were many popular mottoes and slogans expressing both sides of opinion surrounding the conflict. Anti-war protesters wore T-shirts exhorting America to "Make Love, Not War." Pro-war advocates displayed bumper stickers advising, "America: Love It or Leave It!" One of the more popular slogans of that era forced a bit of philosophical reflection. On posters, T-shirts, and bumper stickers across America, it asked, "What if they gave a war and nobody came?" Perhaps that was an option with Vietnam, but it is certainly not an option with the war you and I are engaged in.

Like it or not, you and I are in an epic and lifelong war that affects every area of our lives. For many, the motto of this war could be "What if you were in a war and didn't even know it?" The war is often remarkably subtle. Many men and women are casualties of a war they didn't even know was being waged. This is not to be the case for you and me. We are to be conscious of the reality of spiritual warfare. We are to be prepared and equipped to wage this war. Jesus expects that His followers will emerge from this conflict victorious. To this end, Jesus taught the disciples

> **"Like it or not, you and I are in an epic and lifelong war that affects every area of our lives. For many, the motto of this war could be 'What if you were in a war and didn't even know it?'"**

that one of the seven major components of their prayer was to be a time of developing spiritual protection. He taught us to pray, "Lead us not into temptation, but deliver us from evil" (Matthew 6:13, KJV).

THE INTERNAL ENEMY

Jesus' instruction in the Lord's Prayer regarding our need for spiritual protection identifies the two greatest enemies we face in spiritual warfare. He first instructed the disciples to pray, "Lead us not into temptation." It's hard for most of us to come to the realization that, in fact, a part of our very nature is our enemy, the part of our nature that is so attracted to temptation.

In the seventh chapter of the book of Romans, the Apostle Paul paints a vivid picture of our internal struggle. In the crucial verse of this text Paul declares, "I know that nothing good dwells in me, that is, in my flesh" (v. 18, NASB). When Paul speaks of flesh here, he is not referring to the physical flesh of the human anatomy. He is speaking about an internal propensity toward self-centeredness and sin, which the Bible calls our "old nature." This part of our being was born in a condition which C. S. Lewis, in his novel *Out of the Silent Planet*, referred to as "bent." Almost every internal struggle we face in our spiritual lives is a product of this fallen dimension of our being.

In the fifth chapter of Galatians, Paul enumerated the activities of the flesh: "The acts of the flesh are obvious: sexual immorality, impurity and debauchery; idolatry and witchcraft; hatred, discord, jealousy, fits of rage, selfish ambition, dissensions, factions and envy; drunkenness, orgies, and the like" (vv. 19–21). No wonder Paul tells us in Romans that "those controlled by the flesh cannot please God" (8:8).

Before Jesus Christ came into my life, I only had one nature. That nature was a sin nature. My entire life was under the dominant influence of the flesh. Sinning was easy; it just came naturally. When I invited Christ into my life as Lord and Savior, a wonderful thing happened inside me. The Holy Spirit invaded my life and created a new nature. This new nature is the product of the Holy Spirit's work and presence in my inner life. Now I have the potential to bear the fruit of the Spirit instead of the deeds of the flesh. Notice the difference: "But the fruit of the Spirit is love, joy, peace, patience, kindness, goodness, faithfulness, gentleness and self-control" (Galatians 5:22–23).

Day by day I have the potential of allowing one of these two realities to dominate my life. It is the old sin nature, the

---

"Almost every internal struggle we face in our spiritual lives is a product of this fallen dimension of our being."

---

flesh, that is particularly susceptible to temptation. James notes, "When tempted, no one should say, 'God is tempting me.' For God cannot be tempted by evil, nor does he tempt anyone; but each one is tempted when, by his own evil desire, he is dragged away and enticed" (James 1:13–14).

How do we overcome temptation? God has provided certain resources to help us win this battle. Internalizing the truth of Scripture helps us fight temptation. The psalmist wrote, "I have hidden your word in my heart that I might not sin against you" (Psalm 119:11). Remember, too, that when Jesus was tempted in the wilderness, His consistent response to temptation was "It is written!"

Finding God's way out of temptation can also help us overcome sin. God promises, "No temptation has seized you except what is common to man. And God is faithful; he will not let you be tempted beyond what you can bear. But when you are tempted, he will also provide a way out so that you can stand up under it" (1 Corinthians 10:13).

Sometimes, our way out is to exercise the spiritual will-power I wrote about in chapter 2: to resist the temptation (1 Peter 5:9). At other times, the way out will be to turn from the temptation and flee. At times your flight will be figura-tive (2 Timothy 2:22), and at other times, like Joseph's, it might be literal (Genesis 39:12).

Of all the resources God has provided for overcoming temptation, the most effective is avoidance. That is why we are to pray, "Lead us not into temptation." In a sense, this prayer is answered when, like David, we are able to say, "He leads me in the paths of righteousness for his name's sake" (Psalm 23:3).

During this component of our prayer time, we can begin by praying that God will guide our lives in such a way that we experience a minimum of temptation. In regard to temp-tation, Martin Luther used to say that we can't keep the birds from flying over our heads, but we can keep them from building nests in our hair. Yet, Jesus seems to imply that, in prayer, we might be able to change either the "birds" flight pattern or our exposure to it.

We also can pray that, as God leads us in paths of righ-teousness, He would clothe us in personal holiness. The armor of Ephesians 6 has both defensive and offensive di-mensions. Those pieces that speak metaphorically of de-fense against attack all have to do with our character and lifestyle: "Therefore put on the full armor of God, so that when the day of evil comes, you may be able to stand your ground. . . . Stand firm then, with the belt of *truth* buckled around your waist, with the breastplate of *righteousness* in place. . . . Take up the shield of *faith*, with which you can extinguish all the flaming arrows of the evil one. Take the helmet of *salvation* . . ." (vv. 13–17, emphasis added).

Our prayer closet becomes our "dressing room" as we pray through this dimension of overcoming sin and tempta-tion in our lives.

> **"The first law of spiritual warfare is that Satan hates you and has a diabolical plan for your life."**

THE EXTERNAL ENEMY

The second part of this prayer component is to be focused on Jesus' instruction to pray, "Deliver us from evil" (Matthew 6:13, KJV). The Greek text of the verse includes the definite article before the word *evil*. Literally, the text would be translated "deliver us from *the* evil." Because of the use of the article, many biblical scholars believe Jesus is referring not simply to evil as a principle but rather to evil personified. They would translate this verse (as the NIV does) "deliver us from the evil one."

We not only have an internal enemy, the flesh, in our battle to live the Christian life, but we also have a very real and very personal external enemy. The first law of spiritual warfare is that Satan hates you and has a diabolical plan for your life.

The authority Jesus has given us in prayer is a powerful weapon in overcoming the schemes and attacks of the evil one. I consider praying for God's protection from Satan's attacks one of my greatest privileges and responsibilities.

Over the years, I have grown in my understanding of spiritual warfare. I have also grown in my understanding and experience of the resources I have been given in Christ to deal with Satan's schemes. I have come to understand something of the authority God has given the Christian to stand and exercise authority in the face of evil, and the invitation He has given us to pray for spiritual protection against Satan's ever gaining access to our lives.

SPIRITUAL PROTECTION

Many years ago, I attended a series of seminars called "The Institute in Basic Youth Conflicts," taught by Bill Gothard. Bill developed an illustration of the father's spiritual authority in the family. A picture of an umbrella represented the father's protective authority. When members of the family moved out from under the father's authority in rebellion or disobedience, they also moved out from underneath this umbrella of protection and became more susceptible to satanic attacks. When the father was out of fellowship with the Father, either through sin or negligence, his umbrella developed holes, making it possible for Satan to gain access more easily to those under the father's authority. How do we put up a spiritual umbrella of protection? I believe we pray it into place. When we are instructed to pray, "Deliver us," the word used in the Greek text is *rhuomai*. It means not only "deliver from" but also "preserve from," or "protect from."

The Bible gives many vivid images of God's providing spiritual protection for those who belong to Him. By His presence and His power, He becomes a refuge, or fortress, for those who come to Him for protection (Psalms 27:1–6; 46:1; 91:1–2). As a mother bird protects her children by covering them with her wings, so God provides protective covering to those whom He loves (Psalm 91:4).

One of the more vivid images of God's provision of supernatural protection is found in Job, the oldest book of the Bible. We are told that Job was an upright man who walked with God. In the unseen realm of heavenly realities, God and Satan discussed Job (1:6–8). Satan, desiring to afflict Job with destruction, made note of the fact that God had erected a figurative hedge around Job, his household, and everything Job had (vv. 9–10). Job's story is a story of God's removing that hedge and allowing Satan to attack Job. God allowed Job to suffer temporarily so that he could grow spiritually and be enlightened for all eternity.

The image of a hedge surrounding Job's life is a useful one in our prayer time. Since the historical setting of both the Old and New Testaments is agricultural, agricultural

---

"God allowed Job to suffer temporarily so that he could grow spiritually and be enlightened for all eternity."

---

images helped to convey God's message to the initial recipients. When a farmer planted a vineyard in Israel, he built a hedge around it to keep foxes, pests, and other destructive predators out of the vineyard. God often described Israel as His vineyard. He built a spiritual hedge around Israel to protect the nation. When Israel slipped into idolatry and immorality by worshiping the gods of other nations, God removed His hedge; and the nation was attacked and ravaged. In Isaiah's "Song of the Vineyard" (Isaiah 5:1–7), God warned Israel that He was about to send judgment against the nation:

> Now I will tell you
> what I am going to do to my vineyard:
> I will take away its *hedge*,
> and it will be destroyed. (v. 5)

In prayer, you and I can erect a spiritual hedge around our lives and our families. Perhaps the image of a hedge is not as relevant in our technological age as it was in Isaiah's or Job's. I conceptualize a spiritual force field surrounding my life, my family, and my home. This force field is generated by the presence and power of God Himself. In prayer,

I appropriate His spiritual protection against the evil one. I pray a spiritual fortress into place.

THE HOST OF HEAVEN

During this time of prayer, I have also started praying about the ministry of angels in my family's life. I have to admit that I don't understand a lot about angels. Although *This Present Darkness* was not intended to be a theological statement on the ministry of angels, it certainly raised my curiosity. I began to realize how often I breezed right over Bible passages about angelic ministry without giving much thought to what role angels might play in my life. For instance, angelic activity is predominant in the early chapters of the Gospels. Acts 12 tells of Peter's release from prison by angels. And Hebrews 1:14 speaks of "ministering spirits."

Since one of the *YHWH* names of God is Lord of the Host, I have simply started to pray that God would release the angels appointed to minister to our family and that the host of heaven would be a part of our spiritual defense system.

When I have finished this component of prayer, I find that I am able to face the day with a sense of confidence and peace that I have responsibly exercised the authority I have been entrusted with to appropriate divine protection for my family in our spiritual warfare.

When this component of prayer has been completed, I have prayed through all of my "us" issues. I am now ready to focus once again on God Himself and address the final issues of the Lord's Prayer.

ASSIGNMENT 1: WEEK SEVEN

1. Add a section to your prayer notebook entitled "Spiritual Protection" (Appendix A, p. 179).

2. Under "Spiritual Protection," list the areas in which you are especially susceptible to temptation and failure.

3. Make a list of the qualities Paul identifies as part of your spiritual armor in Ephesians 6:10–20.

4. Write out a section on building a spiritual fortress. Make note of the presence and power of God as the source of deliverance from the evil one.

5. Ask the Holy Spirit to help you pray for thirty minutes, five days this week.

6. Pray, using the six components developed in your notebook so far.

WEEK SEVEN:

FINAL ISSUES

_____ Eleven

"YOURS IS THE KINGDOM"

In Al-Anon's daily reading book, *One Day At a Time In Al-Anon*, the reading for June 14 begins with the following question: "If someone were to say to me: 'Here is a medicine that can change your whole life for the better; it will put you in a state of relaxed serenity; help you overcome the nagging undercurrent of guilt for past errors, give you new insight into yourself and your spiritual value, and let you meet life's challenges with confidence and courage,' would I take it?"

If you wouldn't answer that question in the affirmative, you probably need to check in at your local mental health hospital. Although, in context, the question refers to the program of AA and Al-Anon, it is exactly the question we need to ask ourselves about the practice of prayer. Obviously, prayer takes more work and self-discipline than taking medicine, or everyone would pray. Ironically, no medicine can give you lasting serenity, insight, or spiritual growth because the work and self-discipline required in prayer are crucial in producing growth. "No pain, no gain" is just as true in the prayer closet as it is in the weight room and gym.

TRANSLATING RESOLVE INTO ACTION

Last year, one of the top sporting goods companies popularized a slogan:

—— *Just Do It!* ——

The slogan is a call to renounce the life of a couch potato and to begin to exercise. In the discipline of prayer, we need to cultivate the same motto:

—— *Just Do It!* ——

For most of us, the breakdown comes here. We need to translate our resolve into action. As we come to the end of our study of the Lord's Prayer, we will face this hurdle. Knowing what we know, will we now continue (or start) a regular time of significant prayer?

Recently, a good friend of mine returned from the Cooper Clinic in Dallas, Texas. Dr. Cooper and his staff run one of the leading heart clinics in the world, specializing in heart disease recovery and heart attack recovery. While my friend was there, the doctors helped him to develop an exercise program designed to prolong his life and help prevent heart attack. I found one of their instructions relevant to prayer. My friend was not only given an exercise program to follow; he was told that he needed to develop a habit of using it. He was told that, to develop a habit, he needed to exercise at least five times a week. Studies have shown that, if we set a goal of exercising only three days a week, it becomes too easy to make excuses and fail to *Just Do It!* In contrast, when we set a goal of five days a week, we are less likely to put off our exercise. Five days a week develops a habit.

I found this information fascinating, because that has proven true in my prayer life. My personal goal has been to have a significant time of prayer at least five days a week. Often, five becomes seven, because the habit has become ingrained. If I miss a day, I know I need to get back on the program the next day. If I am only shooting for three days a week, my tendency to put off till tomorrow what I need to do today will take over.

As we come to the end of our study, I want to encourage you:

—— *Just Do It!* ——

And just do it at least five days a week. Building a physical discipline of exercising five days a week will strengthen your heart and prolong your life. But building a discipline of praying significantly five days a week will actually change your heart and transform the quality of your life.

THE PERFECT PATTERN

Many people never get in shape, because they don't know what to do or how to get going. For many, a simple, workable program that is easy to understand makes the difference between becoming healthy or staying unfit. Learning how to start slowly and build gradually plays a critical role in finally getting in shape.

In the practice of prayer, the same dynamics apply. Many of us respond to emotional appeals that we need to pray more, but we don't know how to start. We might even set unrealistic goals for ourselves and then grow discouraged when we fail to keep those goals. Hopefully, this book has been of some help in overcoming both of those difficulties. If you simply follow the weekly assignments, you will start very slowly and build up over the weeks to significant times of prayer. When you're praying and are tempted to stop, check the clock first, and push yourself to keep the schedule. As we have looked closely at each component of the Lord's Prayer, we have attempted to put together a strategy that will make prayer meaningful and significant for us. Now the time has come to become men and women of prayer.

As you look back over the components, I hope you can see that Jesus has given us the perfect pattern for prayer. I think it is safe to suggest that Christ Himself worked through the seven components when He prayed. Let's review.

Component One: "Father"

I began my time of prayer by focusing on my relationship with the living God. This was a time of consciously entering His presence as I remembered and reflected on the truth that He is my *abba*, daddy, papa, through my relationship with Jesus Christ. I entered His presence with a sense of powerlessness, calling on the person of the Holy Spirit to help me pray as He has promised He would.

As I entered His presence, I asked for this time of prayer to be a time of true intimacy and real spiritual fellowship with God, the Father.

I also focused on Jesus Christ. I reaffirmed that, in this prayer time, I would surrender to His lordship in my life. I remembered that, when I belong to Him, He calls me "friend." I prayed that this time of prayer would lead me into the experience of His friendship.

I thanked God that in my powerlessness and the un-manageability of my life created by that powerlessness, He is there to bring sanity, serenity, power, and fruitfulness to my day.

Component Two: "Hallowed Be Your Name"

Having spent adequate time praying about my relationship with God, I then began to seek His face in a time of prayerful worship. I used His name and names to remind me of all the wonderful dimensions of who He is. In praise and thanksgiving, I contemplated, reflected on, and appropriated who He

---

"Building a physical discipline of exercising five days a week will strengthen your heart and prolong your life. But building a discipline of praying significantly five days a week will actually change your heart and transform the quality of your life."

---

is. I entered "his gates with thanksgiving and his courts with praise" (Psalm 100:4). During this time of worship, I set my heart and mind on God's agenda and allowed the Holy Spirit to bring my spirit into harmony with His.

Component Three: "Thy Kingdom Come . . . Thy Will Be Done"

In light of who God is and as a response to my time of worship and praise, I then asked for the Holy One to intervene in my daily life. I spent time appropriating divine intervention. I recognized and rejoiced in God's delight in my desire to have Him intervene and bring heavenly realities to bear on earthly situations. I asked Him to bring the power of His kingdom to bear on my life for that day. I asked Him to intervene on behalf of my family, my church, my city, my nation, and the world. I prayed through all the areas in which I long to see His will done on earth as it is in heaven.

Component Four: "Give Us This Day Our Daily Bread"

Having adequately prayed about God's agenda and having spent time focusing my attention on Him, I then prayed about my specific needs. I came to God, my Father, who is *Jehovah-jireh*, and looked to Him to provide my daily bread. I asked. I asked for my physical needs to be met. I asked for my emotional needs to be met. I asked for my spiritual needs to be met. I prayed about the issues of the day that constitute my daily bread.

Recognizing that many of my anxieties in life are related to wants rather than needs, I prayed about the areas that cause me anxiety. I prayed that I would learn to live in God's kingdom provision with contentment and that I would meet all the conditions attached to His provision.

Component Five: "Forgive Us Our Sins"

Having prayed for my physical needs, I also spent some time appropriating the forgiveness and cleansing of Christ's atonement. I acknowledged before my heavenly Father that I am a sinner constantly in need of His mercy and grace. I gave thanks that Jesus' death on the cross provided full and free forgiveness for my moral, ethical, and spiritual failure. I allowed the Holy Spirit to reveal to me any actions, attitudes, or thoughts that I needed to confess. I experientially received God's forgiveness and cleansing.

After experiencing forgiveness in my own life, I thought of any people in my life who had offended me since my last prayer time. If I was harboring any bitterness or resentment,

I confessed my sin and then made a conscious choice to forgive the one who had sinned against me.

Component Six: "Lead Us Not into Temptation"

In prayer, I have erected a spiritual fortress around my life and around my family. I have asked the Lord to keep me away from temptation. I have prayed that my life would be clothed in the armor of personal holiness, biblical humility,

> **"I have found that, at times, the delight goes away, and prayer becomes pure discipline again. I have also found that, at times, discipline must overcome the lack of desire."**

and spiritual authority. I have asked that, by His presence and with His power, the Holy One would place a hedge around my home and my family. I have asked that He would cover us with His protective presence. I have prayed that the host of heaven would be active in their ministry to my family this day.

Component Seven: Final Affirmations

By the time I reach the final component of prayer, I have had a great time with the Lord. When I first began using this pattern in April 1989, I remembered Dr. Lea talking about his progression through the transformation of his own prayer life. Using an alliterative device (as all good preachers must), he spoke of moving from the *desire* to pray, into the *discipline* of prayer, and finally experiencing the *delight* of prayer. My own experience has been a little different. I have found that, at times, the delight goes away, and prayer becomes pure discipline again. I have also found that, at times, discipline must overcome the lack of desire. But often, the delight returns, and always I have the satisfaction of obedience in my prayer walk. Usually, if I can just get past the first hurdle of actually beginning to pray through the pattern, the desire returns.

The final component Jesus taught the disciples to pray was an affirmation that seems to be a totally logical way to end our time of prayer. As we wind down our prayer time, we confess and affirm that "Yours is the kingdom." This affirmation flows freely when we have experienced God's presence during prayer. It is a blessing to be able to affirm that, in the midst of the craziness around us, a higher reality is ours. The kingdoms of this world are fading and passing away. The only true and lasting kingdom is the kingdom of God. Our God reigns! He is still on the throne. The destiny of the universe and of our lives is in His hands. I am reminded that Jesus encouraged the disciples, "Do not be afraid, little flock, for your Father has been pleased to give you the kingdom" (Luke 12:32). I end my prayer time confident that, this day, I can live a kingdom lifestyle flowing out of my relationship with God.

We are to further affirm, "Yours is the power." I began my prayer time by acknowledging my own powerlessness. It is appropriate to end by acknowledging God's omnipotence. His is the power! As He has done with the kingdom, He has been pleased to make His power available to me. Through prayer, I have tapped into the power source; and I'm ready to face the day living in the power of the Holy Spirit.

Finally, we are to affirm, "Yours is the glory." The first question in the Westminster Confession's catechism asks, "What is the chief end of man?" We might put the question in more contemporary terms: "What is the purpose of life?"

The answer is both simple and profound: "The chief end of man is to glorify God and enjoy Him forever." All I say, all I do, all I think, and all I am are to bring glory to the living God. I am being transformed into the image of Christ with ever-increasing glory, that my life might bring glory to God (2 Corinthians 3:18).

A PERFECT STRATEGY

It is a perfect pattern: seven components given to the disciples by the perfect Teacher. When developed and followed in prayer, it provides a perfect strategy for transforming our prayer life. If we will allow Christ to use it in our lives, we can become men and women of the most powerful force on earth: prayer! So remember:

—— *Just Do It!* ——

ASSIGNMENT 2: WEEK SEVEN

1. Review all the previous assignments.

2. Complete your prayer notebook by adding a page for final affirmations.

3. Ask the Holy Spirit to help you pray thirty minutes, five days this week.

4. Pray: *Just do it!*

WEEK SEVEN:

THE FINAL FRONTIER

Twelve

BEYOND THE LORD'S PRAYER

B y the time you get to this chapter, you might be saying to yourself, "No more!" I certainly can understand your sentiment. On the other hand, you might also be thinking, "Wait a minute, what about . . . ?" Even though I have covered a lot of turf in the preceding chapters, there are still facets of prayer that I have hardly touched on.

PRAYER 101

To put what we have and haven't explored into perspective, you might think of this book as a beginning course in prayer. We have just covered Prayer 101. I'm convinced that those of us who are just getting started on the prayer journey have many exciting years ahead of us discovering the many exciting facets of prayer God has made available. I was recently reading Teresa of Avila on prayer. She used the image of an inner castle to teach about the cultivation of inner spiritual life. I began to realize that we have the privilege of building the inner castle through our time alone with God. I believe that I have often had a minuscule conception of the human heart. When we speak of Jesus living in our hearts, I usually conceptualize some small place within the confines of my physical being. Without thinking about it, I have viewed this place as a small box no bigger than my physical heart. In reality, our hearts have the possibility of nearly infinite development. I'm sure that Teresa of Avila actually possessed an inner castle built in the quiet of her times alone with God. While we are praying, God is building. Many of our inner lives are little more than shacks. As we pray, God will change that.

Several years ago, Robert Munger published a classic booklet entitled *My Heart, Christ's Home*. The booklet graphically pictures the different areas of our inner lives as rooms in a house. Munger was encouraging us to meet day by day with Christ in the library and to turn over every room, closet, nook, and cranny to His lordship. Jesus not only wants to occupy our house as is, He also has blueprints for the addition of new rooms. He wants to build a mansion, then a castle, then a city, then a whole inner world where He reigns. His intention is that our inner worlds and inner lives would be so rich that our preoccupation with and love of the material world would fade by comparison.

Shortly after I began praying through the pattern in this book, I took off on a cross-country motorcycle trip with a group of my friends. We had been planning the trip and anticipating our adventure for nearly a year. We flew to Milwaukee, Wisconsin, the birthplace of Harley Davidson motorcycles, where twenty-five men in our group picked up new Harley Davidson motorcycles. Five of us who already owned bikes shipped our cycles on a truck so that we could ride with the group. We rode through Wisconsin, Minnesota, South Dakota, and the Black Hills, and out to Yellowstone National Park. Some days, the weather was perfect. Other days, we rode through thunderstorms and high winds. It was quite an adventure.

Early in the trip, I had an important insight. I wasn't enjoying the trip as much as I had anticipated. I tried to get a handle on why. Suddenly, I began to think about the other exciting adventure I had been on over the last few months. I had been regularly "traveling" into the presence of God. I had been spending hours building my inner cas-

---

"His intention is that our inner worlds and inner lives would be so rich that our preoccupation with and love of the material world would fade by comparison."

---

tle. I began to realize that the richness of my inner journey had actually eclipsed the excitement of my outer journey. Nothing that we can experience in the physical world will ever give us the joy of our experience in the presence of God. David said it perfectly in the psalms when under the inspiration of the Holy Spirit, he wrote, "In Your *presence* is fullness of joy" (Psalm 16:11, NKJV, emphasis added). We all long for fullness of joy. And it is found only in the presence of the Lord. While we are clothed in these mortal bodies, the only way to enter the presence of the Lord is in prayer.

ADVANCED PRAYER

After we have started to develop a more meaningful time of prayer, using the pattern Jesus has given us, we might find ourselves wondering where to go from here. Other dimensions of prayer that are not explicitly spelled out in the

Lord's Prayer have been significant in the prayer lives of men and women of prayer throughout the ages.

Over the years, I have come to appreciate the great diversity of God's creative genius in the way He has made each of us unique. This uniqueness will definitely appear in the unfolding development of our prayer lives. Some of us have been created and shaped with logical and thinking-dominant personalities. Others of us are "wired" in more feeling and intuition-oriented ways. As our spiritual lives develop, these inherent distinctions will shape our relationships with God. For some of us, nothing brings the reality of God's presence into our experience quite like a good time of Bible study. All our logic circuits get filled with truth, and the Holy One's presence comes alive to us. For others, sitting quietly to contemplate the sunset over the mountains ushers them right into the presence of the Lord. Some of us are more mystical. Others are not. As our prayer lives develop, we will need to discover individually what dimensions of prayer are most effective for us.

The Lord's Prayer provides a perfect framework for exploring and developing these other dimensions of prayer.

Contemplation and Meditation

If you analyze the approach to the Lord's Prayer in this book, you will see that it is filled with specific content and active prayer. Within the body of Christ, certain circles have placed renewed emphasis on a much different approach to prayer. Some from these circles might read this book and ask where the quiet listening part of prayer is reflected in these instructions. They might point us to the text in the Old Testament where God encourages us, "Be still and know that I am God" (Psalm 46:10).

Mature prayer is definitely not a monologue. It is an encounter with the living God, who wants to communicate with us. True prayer is a dialogue of two. Therefore, as we grow in our prayer time, we need to learn to listen. This listening dimension is emphasized by those who practice a more contemplative form of prayer.

There are certain difficulties with finding an appropriate practice of contemplative prayer. Much has been written about this subject, both by those who advocate the practice

---

"The emptying of the mind is a dangerous activity. Something will move into the vacuum. Often, I fear, the very demonic presence being called on by the chanting creates the spiritual experience in the life of the one meditating."

---

and those who find it counterproductive. The negative critiques center on the similarities between certain practices advocated in contemplative prayer and meditation and those expressed by New Age and Eastern religious gurus. We need to walk in a discerning and biblically discriminating way. It is possible to get rid of the bath water without throwing out the baby.

To simplify a very complex subject, often the difference between Christian meditation and Eastern meditation has to do with what is in our heads as we meditate. Eastern meditation advocates an emptying of the mind. From a purely physiological perspective, the chanting of a mantra occupies the lower functions of the brain so that the logic centers are kept inoperative. The same physiological phenomenon could be achieved by chanting something like "bunk" over and over again just as easily as the chanting of the name of a Hindu deity. The emptying of the mind is a dangerous activity. Something will move into the vacuum. Often, I fear, the very demonic presence being called on by the chanting creates the spiritual experience in the life of the one meditating.

New Age meditation is difficult to define. Much of it involves visualization, which ranges all the way from visualizing pleasant and peaceful landscapes to the visualization of spirit guides, who are invited to come into one's consciousness and guide one's life. From a biblical perspective, the latter practice opens the door to tremendous spiritual deception. These practices are not without real experience and apparent benefit. But the dangers to which practitioners of these disciplines are oblivious do concern biblical Christians.

It is important to recognize that certain forms of meditation and even visualization long preceded the current faddish, and often occultic, versions practiced by certain New Age groups today. The biblical mandate to seek the face of God seems to have a visual dimension. The Holy Spirit can bring us powerful images of ourselves folded in the arms of a loving God or being touched by the healing hand of Jesus.

Christian contemplation and meditation seek not to empty the mind but to fill it. Over time, as we hallow the name of God, we will find it incredibly significant to take time to contemplate God's excellencies revealed in His name. We meditate on His truth and His person as revealed to us in Scripture. We learn to be still and sit quietly in His presence as the Holy Spirit comes alive in our experience through prayer. As we quietly reflect and meditate in prayer, He will speak to us significantly—even if we are not mystical by nature.

Intercession

Shortly after I developed my prayer outline and began to pray through the Lord's Prayer, I became aware that I still needed to pray for many people and about many issues.

Earlier, I had kept a prayer list of the needs of others I had been asked to pray for. I found it difficult to be consistent in praying for those needs. In praying through the Lord's Prayer, however, I am much more effective in praying for people and situations that need intercession.

There are two approaches to building our ministry of intercession. One is simply to incorporate these needs into our existing outline. For you, it might prove beneficial to develop a list of people and needs for intercession and place it with your time of appropriating divine intervention. I think you recognize that, during that time, you are already exercising intercessory prayer.

I have found it more helpful personally to keep a separate list in my notebook and to have special times of pure intercession (Appendix A, p. 173). My list includes friends in ministry, my actual physical neighbors, friends, family, and special needs that I have been asked to pray for. I also keep a special page that I call my "Miracle List."

I know and believe that God can do anything. The message of the incarnation is that "nothing is impossible with God" (Luke 1:37). In the Old Testament book of Jeremiah, God offers an invitation: "Call to me and I will answer you and tell you

---

"We learn to be still and sit quietly in His presence as the Holy Spirit comes alive in our experience through prayer."

---

great and unsearchable things you do not know" (33:3).

God gave this invitation when the city of Jerusalem was under siege by the Babylonian army. Shortly, the city would be destroyed and the people who survived would be carried into captivity. Yet, God promised that a day would come when He would bring healing, forgiveness, and cleansing to Israel (vv. 6–9). Out of this redemption would come a rebuilding that would produce abundant prosperity and peace. God was going to do the impossible for Israel!

There is a New Testament parallel to this great Old Testament invitation. The Apostle Paul ends the third chapter of Ephesians with a benediction, which includes the following phrase: "Now to him who is able to do immeasurably more than all we ask or imagine . . ." (v. 20).

I have written these two Scripture texts above my Miracle List (Appendix A, p. 173). Under them, I have written the phrase *Impossible apart from intervention by the living God!* Under this phrase I have listed needs I pray for that appear to be completely impossible, or at least so difficult that they will require God's special intervention. For instance, one of my friends has a son born with a seriously deformed leg. The entire bottom part of his leg was missing, leaving him with half a leg. He has been through a series of very painful surgeries to help him use a prosthesis. My heart goes out to this little guy. He has more spirit and courage than any pro in the National Football League. I pray that God will grow him a leg. I believe God can do it. I don't know if God will do it now (one day He definitely will). But I do know that He is the God who turns hard rock into springs of water (Psalm 114:8) and who does whatever pleases Him (Psalm 115:3).

I have already had the joy of seeing some of the items on my miracle list answered. Others may not be answered until Christ returns, but I consider it a great privilege to pray for the impossible.

THE FINAL FRONTIER

I guess I have to make one final confession. I am a Trekkie. I can't help it, I love those pointed ears on Mr. Spock. I am tempted almost every Sunday to end the worship service by flashing the Vulcan "V" sign and pronouncing the benediction: "Live long and prosper!" It just seems so biblical! Each episode of this classic television show began with the same teaser: "Space, the final frontier."

Space is not really the final frontier. The real final frontier is the world of the spirit. Space is finite. One day, we might actually master space. It seems improbable given the vastness of the universe, but it is possible. But the realm of the spirit is infinite. It will provide an eternity of unimaginable adventure and excitement. God delights in our desire to explore this frontier. He has given us a map to guide us on our adventure. He also promises to be with us on our journey. When all on Earth is said and done, we will find that He, Himself, is the journey. To know Him, love Him, serve Him, and enjoy Him forever—that is eternal life. For now we only see dimly. But our vision can be improved. He waits daily to meet with us. He delights in His children's desire to draw apart from the concerns and activities of the day and speak those words He longs to hear, "Our Father . . ."

ASSIGNMENT 3: WEEK SEVEN

1. Develop a section in your prayer notebook for intercessory prayer.

2. Make a list of people and needs you will pray for regularly.

3. Develop a miracle list. Write out the concerns of your life that require miraculous divine intervention.

4. In prayer this week, attempt to spend time contemplating and quietly meditating on the names of God, the love of God, the cross of Christ, and the work of the Holy Spirit.

5. Ask the Holy Spirit to help you pray.

6. Pray thirty minutes a day, five days this week.

CONCLUSION:

PUTTING IT ALL TOGETHER

Thirteen

SWEET HOUR OF PRAYER

After laboring through the material in the preceding chapters, you still might not be sure how all the components would work in an actual prayer. The following transcript offers an actual hour of prayer executed from the outline of the Lord's Prayer. Please forgive the sloppy grammar and any items that might seem too selfish or repetitious. I am risking a bit by letting you peek into my prayer closet.

I hope you will be gracious and understand that I have a long way to go in learning how to pray. The following is not intended to be some kind of perfect example or model. Your prayer time will probably look quite different. A year from now, I might find that my own time looks quite different. I simply hope this sample will give you an idea of how to put it all together.

PRELIMINARIES   6:47 A.M.

Father . . . I pray for a time of fellowship and prayer this morning. Thank You for this day. Thank You for life. Thank

You that I can wake up and know You are here and You love me.

Romans 8:26–27

Holy Spirit, I ask You to lead me and enable me during this time of prayer. I am powerless over my separation from God, and I don't have the ability to pray apart from Your help. I pray for Your intervention and activation during this time. I ask You to give me an hour of prayer today. According to the promise of God's Word, I ask You to give me persistence, intensity, and tenacity in this time of prayer. Holy Spirit, make this time fruitful, real focused, enjoyable, and experiential. Make this time what the Father wants it to be. Come now, and draw me into the way of the Spirit and into the presence of the Father.

ENTERING HIS PRESENCE

Ephesians 1:17; John 16:27; John 17:23

Father . . . (pause and sit quietly reflecting) *Abba* . . . (pause and reflection) Daddy . . . (pause) . . . Papa . . . draw me into heartfelt intimacy with You today. I pray for the spirit of wisdom and revelation, that I might experientially know You better. Your Word tells me that You love me (both *agape* and *phileo*) just as You love Jesus. Because You have said, "I love you!" let me love You today above all else. I long to live in the daddy-child relationship with You today. Let all that happens today flow from that relationship . . . (pause and brief contemplation).

John 15:14–15; Hebrews 2:11

Lord Jesus, I submit to Your lordship today. You have called me friend. Your Word says that You are not ashamed to call me brother. I pray today that I would experience not only Your lordship over my life but also Your friendship and Your brotherhood in my life.

Ephesians 5:18; Romans 8:15

Holy Spirit, work in my life today. Begin to fill my life with Your presence. Control and empower my life. You are the spirit of adoption that enables me to cry out, *"Abba!"* I pray You would make the spirit of adoption experiential in my life today. Bring into my experience today all that Jesus has purchased by His atonement.

SEEKING HIS FACE   6:54 A.M.

Father . . . Hallowed be thy name. I worship You this morning. I pray that by my lips and through my life You would be honored, exalted, and magnified today. I praise You and bless You. Father, I long to enter Your gates with thanksgiving and Your courts with praise . . . (pause).

Exodus 3:14, Matthew 1:21

I praise You that You are *YHWH*. Lord, You *are* and You *cause to be*. Thank You. I pray that You would be and cause to be in my life today.

I thank You for Your saving grace today. Jesus, I praise You that You are *Ya'shua*, the Lord is Salvation. I thank You for the finished work of the cross. Lord, I would be totally lost if it weren't for You. I thank You that my salvation is finished business. You are holy; You are righteous; You are full of grace, mercy, and love. I praise You and give You thanks.

Jeremiah 23:6; 1 Corinthians 1:30

Thank You, Lord, that You are *YHWH-tsidkenu*. You are righteousness. You are the source of all my righteousness. I confess that I have no righteousness in myself and that all my righteousness is found in You. I thank You that I am in Christ and that You have become my righteousness.

Leviticus 20:8; 1 Corinthians 1:30

Thank You, Lord, that You are *YHWH-m'kaddesh*, the Lord who sanctifies. I desperately need the sanctifying work of Your Holy Spirit to be at work in my life today. I praise You and give You thanks that You are my sanctification positionally and that You are at work in my life to change me and make me pleasing to You.

Ezekiel 48:35; Matthew 28:20; Hebrews 13:5

Thank You, Lord, that You are *YHWH-shamma*. You are present. You are here. Praise You that You are Immanuel: God *with* us. Thank You, Jesus, that You are always with me. Thank You that You will never leave me or forsake me. (Pause and reflect.)

Acts 1:8

Thank You, Holy Spirit, that You are *with* me, and *in* me. I pray that You would come *upon* me with Your anointing touch today. Praise You, Lord, that Your word to me is "I am with you." I am grateful that You are the infinite and omnipresent Lord.

Psalm 23:1; John 10:10

Thank You, Lord, that You are *YHWH-rohi*. You are my Shepherd, Lord, just as You were King David's. Lord, You have guided me, and I give You thanks. I pray today that You would lead me in paths of righteousness. Thank You that You provide for me. You have led me to green pastures and quiet waters. Thank You for Your provision of rest during this time. [This book was written in a three-month sabbatical.] I thank You today that, as my Shepherd, You protect me. Your rod and Your staff comfort me. You are the Good Shepherd. I thank You that, as my Good Shepherd, You are the source of abundant living. I know that Your abundant life is an experience of the kingdom. I pray that You would lead me into kingdom abundance today. You are the source of my security, and I affirm that truth today. Thank You that You are restoring my soul. I give You praise and thanksgiving. I worship You because You are a gracious, loving, and all-powerful Shepherd. . . (pause and worship). (At this point my mind brought the words to consciousness of a praise song:)

> Blessed be Your holy name, Lord Jesus.
> I will never cease to give You praise.
> You are Messiah, Deliverer,
>   the Holy One of Israel.
> Blessed be Your holy name, Lord Jesus.
> I will never cease to give You praise.

Genesis 22:14; Philippians 4:19; Psalm 84:11; James 1:17

Lord, I thank You and worship You that You are *YHWH-jireh*, the source of all my provision. I praise You for Your providence and Your care for my life. Lord Jesus, I thank You for the promise of provision that is part of the new covenant. You are not only my Provider, You are a good Provider. No good thing do You withhold from those who walk uprightly. Every good and perfect gift comes from You.

I praise You and give You thanks that Your provision is rooted in Your all-knowing, all-wise, all-caring, kind nature. I bless You and worship You for Your provision. . . (pause).

Exodus 15:26; Malachi 4:2; James 5:14–15; Isaiah 53:5

I praise You and thank You that You are *YHWH-rophe*, the Lord who heals. Thank You for Your healing touch on our lives. Thank You that You are healing me in my spirit. Praise You, Jesus, that You are the Son of Righteousness who has risen with healing in Your wings. Thank You for Your promise of present healing. Thank You, Lord Jesus, for the healing implications of Your atonement. I thank You for the miracles of healing You have done in Baker's life. I pray that You will continue to heal his eyes and his ears. I pray Your healing power would be at work in the process of his physical and mental development. I pray for Allison that You would continue to heal her hormonal problems, and I ask You to heal her ears and restore her hearing. Thank You, Lord, for Your lovingkindness that makes You care for our infirmities. I praise You, Lord.

Jeremiah 29:11; Galatians 3:13–14; Isaiah 54:17

I give You thanks and praise that You are *YHWH-nissi*, the Lord my Banner. I look to You as the source of victory and success in my life. I thank You for Your promise of a future marked by kingdom prosperity. Thank You, Lord, for freedom from the failure of the curse of the law and the freedom of life in the Spirit. Your banner over my life is love. Because of Your love, I know that no weapon forged against me will prevail. Bless You, Holy Lord! . . (pause for praise).

Judges 6:24; Ephesians 2:14; Galatians 5:22; Galatians 3:14

Thank You that You are *YHWH-shalom*. You are my peace, Lord. You are the source of my well-being, wholeness, harmony, contentment, and satisfaction. Lord, fill me with Your peace. Make me an instrument of Your peace. Lord Jesus, I thank You that You are the source of my peace. Holy Spirit, I praise You that peace is part of the fruit You produce in my life. Thank You that the blessing promised Abraham is now mine in Christ. Thank You that I can live my life under Your covenants. Lord, nothing is more important in my life than living in the center of Your blessing. I praise You and worship You for all You are and all Your name represents. Hallowed, exalted, honored, and magnified be Your name! . . (time of quiet in His presence).

APPROPRIATING DIVINE INTERVENTION 7:13 A.M.

In light of all that You are, Father, I now pray that Your kingdom would come and Your will would be done on earth as it is in heaven. I come to You today and ask for Your divine intervention in my life and the affairs of my life. I am powerless apart from You. Apart from Your intervention my life is unmanageable, unfruitful, frustrating, and chaotic. But I believe You are here, Lord. I believe You have the power to bring sanity, power, and fruitfulness to my life. I turn my will over to Your care today, and I pray that Your will will be done in my life.

John 15:5; Romans 14:17

I pray that Your kingdom would come on my life today. I pray that, by the power of the Holy Spirit, You would bring the reality of the kingdom to bear on the affairs of my life. I choose to relinquish to Your lordship, depend upon Your empowering, and abide in You today. Make my life pleasing to You today. I pray I might see Your face and hear Your voice and see the vision You have for my life. I pray that You would work in my life today to develop spiritual maturity and stature. I pray that, by the ministry of the Holy Spirit, You would work to remove the defects of my character. I pray for Your blessing today, Father. I pray that You would develop my character so that You can prosper and empower my life without corruption. I pray for the kingdom realities of righteousness, peace, and joy in the Holy Spirit to be real in my life today.

Ephesians 5:18; Ephesians 4:22–24

Holy Spirit, fill my life today. Control and empower and guide my life. Make known to me the will of the Father, and give me grace, courage, and power to carry it out. Help me walk in the new man and obey joyfully and willingly. Lead me, Lord. I'm available. Please remove any deceit from my Spirit. Give me a father's heart for my family and the church. Make me an instrument of Your love and Your truth.

Isaiah 61:3

Lord, I pray that Your kingdom would come and Your will would be done in Allison's life today. I pray You would bless her, prosper her, and protect her. I pray You would give her the crown of beauty, the oil of gladness, and the garment of praise. Make her happy, Lord. Give her friends. Bring her helpers. Make her the queen of our house. I pray she would sense great kingdom worth. Holy Spirit, come on our marriage. Minister to her in this time of struggle. Again, I would pray for healing for her ears and full recovery from her surgery. Bless her time with Stephanie and Baker. Bless her, Lord.

Psalm 144:12; Luke 2:52

I pray for Stephanie, that Your kingdom would come on her life today and Your will would be done in her life today. I pray You would bless her, prosper her, and protect her. I pray You would work out Your plans and purposes for her life. Help her grow into a woman of God. Give her inner purity to go with her outer beauty. Protect her from the evil one. Keep her from being defiled by her friends, future boyfriends, her future husband, television, or us. Help her grow in wisdom and stature, and in favor with You and with people. I pray she would be a kingdom kid. Help her with her reading, writing, and math skills so that she would be up to speed with her class this year.

Luke 2:52

I pray for Baker, that Your kingdom would come on him and Your will would be done in his life. Bless him, prosper him, and protect him. Give him health, nurture, strength, and peace according to the promises of Your Word. I again pray for his eyes and ears and physical development. I pray that You would help him grow to be a man of God and a diplomat of the kingdom. Help him grow in wisdom and stature, and in favor with You and with men. I pray for Your divine intervention in our family and that You would be glorified in our family.

I pray that Your kingdom would come and Your will would be done in our church, Lord. Bless the church, Lord. Prosper and protect the church. Bring renewal, revival, and reformation to the church. I pray for the elders, that You would give them wisdom to govern the church. As we face the decisions about the future, I pray You will make Your will known to us. (Individually prayed for each of the eleven elders.) I pray for Jim today. Bless him and keep him renewed and refreshed. Prosper his life and his ministry. I pray for Matt today. Thanks for his help. I pray You would bless his life and ministry today. I pray for Dutch. Give him wisdom as he works to bring more order to the staff. Help us find Your balance between freedom and wise management. I pray for Tom. Thanks for his friendship. Bless his life and ministry today. Thanks for Schultzie, Lord. Bless him today. Protect and bless our staff, Father.

I pray for our ministry in the city. Build up our body in maturity. Work in the lives of those You have chosen to come to know You through our ministry. Bring in the harvest, Lord. Provide a place for us that will enable us to fulfill the ministry You have planned for us. If it would be pleasing to You, I pray that we might be a breakthrough church, a power-point church, a net to catch the harvest. Make us a weapon forged for Your kingdom.

I pray for our city today, Lord. I pray that You would move on Denver, by the power of the Holy Spirit, to bring revival. Break the bonds of wickedness that restrain the fruitfulness of the gospel in Denver.

I pray for Detroit today, Lord. Break through the spiritual resistance to the gospel that is at work in that city.

I pray for our state today, Lord. I pray for Terry (state senator). Bless his life and use him to work for righteousness.

2 Chronicles 7:14

I pray for our nation today, Lord. I pray for Your mercy for our land and Your forgiveness. I pray You will heal our land and send a movement of the Holy Spirit to bring revival to our nation. I pray for President Bush today. Minister to him today. Be at work in his life as he faces the crisis in Iraq. Bless Bill (United States senator) as he comes to the end of his term. I pray for his health today. I pray his successor would be a righteous person.

I pray for the world today, Lord. I pray for world hunger: provide food. I pray for peace in the world. I pray that the world would be effectively evangelized by 2000. I pray for Germany today. Move by the power of Your spirit there. I pray for the ministry in Estonia. Keep working as You have. Bless Endel and his work there. I pray for India. Bless the ministries of Josh, P. G., George, and Paul. I pray for a great harvest through their lives and ministries. Bless their lives and families and meet their needs. I pray for Wes and Gertie in France. Give them a great harvest of converts from Islam. I pray for Leroy and Kathy in Senegal. Bless them and make their ministry fruitful.

PRAYING FOR PROVISION   7:38 A.M.

Matthew 6:33

Father, give us this day our daily bread. Thank You that You are *YHWH-jireh,* the source of all our provision. I thank You today for this day's bread. I thank You that You have met our material provision. I pray that You would continue to provide the financial resources to meet our needs. Keep us seeking Your kingdom and making Your kingdom our ultimate priority. I know You will add to our lives all we need. Give that we can give, Lord.

Psalm 35:27

I pray for biblical prosperity today. I am Your servant, Lord. You delight in the prosperity of Your servant. Help us be faithful to meet the conditions attached to Your provision.

Today I pray for my emotional and spiritual "daily bread." I pray that, as this time of sabbatical comes to an end, You would complete the process of refreshing, renewing, and restoring me. Make this a good day of rest and renewal.

Help me be a wise and faithful manager of the resources You have given me.

Philippians 4:6; Psalm 106:15

Father, You always meet my *needs*. I now bring before You some of the wants and anxieties of my life. I pray that those things that would be a part of Your will You would do. I also pray that, if any of these requests or desires would bring leanness into my soul, that You would graciously not grant them.

I ask today that You would either raise up a buyer for our house or provide us with the resources to finish and maintain the house. I ask that You might work so that we would know one way or the other what we should do by the end of the summer.

I ask You to work in our car situation. Give me wisdom about what to do. Thank You for the sale of the motorcycle. I pray You would raise up buyers for the cars and lead me in what to replace them with.

Thank You for a great week of vacation in Kansas City. I pray You would work out the details of the possible trip to Disney World in February.

Help me build a responsible savings.

Help me be faithful in my giving.

I pray You would provide for the kids' college education. If possible, I pray they would be able to go to Westmont.

Provide healthy food today and help me make healthy choices.

I ask You to help me get my book written and I pray You would provide a publisher.

Lead Ali and me into relationships that will provide meaningful fellowship and friendships. . . (other personal needs and desires prayed through).

EXPERIENCING FORGIVENESS   7:41 A.M.

Psalm 32:1–5; 1 John 1:9

Lord, I confess today that I am a sinner constantly in need of Your grace and forgiveness. By nature I am restless, irritable, and discontented. I ask You to work to replace those states with peace, joy, and a grateful heart. I confess the sinful defects of my nature. I confess my lust, greed, anger, insecurity, self-centeredness, meanness, and harshness. I ask You to work by the power of the Holy Spirit to remove these defects of character and make me more like Jesus. I confess my critical spirit toward Allison yesterday as sin and pray for Your forgiveness and cleansing. I confess my impatience with Stephanie yesterday as sin. . . (quiet time to allow Spirit to reveal sin).

I pray that You would enable me to treat any offense against me today with forgiveness. To the best of my ability, I am not aware of any bitterness or unforgiveness I am harboring. If I am, I ask You to reveal it to me. Help me remember that bitterness doesn't hurt the other person, it hurts me.

Show me anyone I have offended and need to make amends to. . . (pause). Keep my life free from the accumulated crud of unconfessed sin. Thank You for Your grace and cleansing power.

BUILDING A SPIRITUAL FORTRESS   7:45 A.M.

Ephesians 6:12–14

Father, lead us not into temptation today. Deliver us from all the schemes and attacks of the evil one. I pray that You would keep me away from the attraction and seduction of sin today. Teach me the lessons I need to learn in some other way. Clothe me in the spiritual armor of righteousness, truthfulness, integrity, and humility.

Job 1:10; Hebrews 1:14; Ephesians 2:6

I ask You to build a spiritual "hedge" around our lives and our home today. By Your power and Your presence, protect our lives from the destructive attacks of the evil one. Cover us with Your presence and release the host of heaven to come and surround our lives today. You are my refuge and fortress. Protect me today. Help me to live out of the reality of my position in the heavenlies and to exercise the spiritual authority You have vested me with.

FINAL ISSUES   7:47 A.M.

Luke 12:32

Lord, I rejoice that I can affirm today that Yours is the kingdom. I thank You that You have freely chosen to give me the kingdom. Help me live a kingdom lifestyle today.

Ephesians 3:16

I affirm, Lord, that Yours is the power. In all of my powerlessness, I pray that You would strengthen me with power in my inner man today.

2 Corinthians 3:18

I affirm that Yours is the glory. Transform me into Your image with ever-increasing glory, so that my life might bring glory to You today. *Amen.*

[From here, if time and leading allowed I would move on to pray through my lists of special intercessory prayer requests and my Miracle List.]

PRAYER NOTEBOOK

PRAYER NOTEBOOK	
Topic	**Scriptures**
I. Entering His Presence: *"Father"*	Matthew 6:9
A. Commitment and promise: "By Your grace and with Your help I will be a man (or woman) of prayer."	Psalms 109:4 Haggai 2:19
B. Preliminaries: (my powerlessness)	
1. Appropriating the Holy Spirit's help	Romans 8:26–27
a. Intervention	Romans 8:26–27
b. Enablement	Romans 8:26–27
c. Focus	Romans 8:26–27
d. Fruitfulness	Romans 8:26–27
e. Time: "Help me pray ____ minutes today."	Romans 8:26–27
2. Renewing my relationship	
a. Father—*Abba*	
(1) Intimacy (heartfelt)	Ephesians 1:17
(2) Love (*agape* and *phileo*)	John 16:27
(3) Sonship (walk-in)	Romans 8:15–16
b. Son—Jesus	
(1) Lordship	John 20:28
(2) Friendship	John 15:15
(3) Brotherhood	Hebrews 2:11
c. Spirit—Holy Spirit	
(1) The way of the Spirit	Galatians 5:16, 25
(2) Experience of adoption	Galatians 4:6, 7
II. Seeking His Face: *"Hallowed Be Your Name."*	Matthew 6:9
"Enter His gates with thanksgiving and his courts with praise" (honor, exalt, magnify)	Psalms 100:4
A. Exalt His name . . . *YHWH*	Psalms 138:2
1. I Am	Exodus 3:14

PRAYER NOTEBOOK	
Topic	**Scriptures**
2. I Cause to Be	Psalms 135:6
B. Praise His names	
1. The Lord is Salvation	Psalms 27:1
a. *Ya'Shua*—"Jesus"	Matthew 1:21
b. *YHWH-tsidkenu*—"the Lord is Righteousness"	Jeremiah 23:6
c. *YHWH-m'kaddesh*—"the Lord who sanctifies"	Leviticus 20:8 1 Corinthians 1:30
2. The Lord is present	
a. *YHWH-shamma*—"the Lord is present"	Ezekiel 48:35
b. *Immanuel*—"God with us"	Matthew 1:23
c. Promise of the presence	Matthew 28:20; John 14:18; Hebrews 13:5
d. Ministry of the Holy Spirit: with, in, and upon	John 14:17
e. "I am with you":—*YHWH*	Haggai 1:13
3. The Lord is Shepherd	Psalms 23:1–6
a. *YHWH-rohi*—my Shepherd	Psalms 23:1
(1) Provider—green pastures, quiet waters	Psalms 23:2
(2) Guide—paths of righteousness	Psalms 23:3
(3) Protector—His rod and staff	Psalms 23:4
(4) Restorer—of my soul	Psalms 23:3
b. Good Shepherd	John 10:10
c. Source of my security	Psalms 3:5–6
4. The Lord is Provider	

Appendix A

PRAYER NOTEBOOK	
Topic	**Scriptures**
a. *YHWH-jireh*—"the Lord will provide"	Genesis 22:14
b. Promise of provision	Philippians 4:19
c. Good Provider and provider of good	Psalms 84:11 James 1:17
5. The Lord is Healer	
a. *YHWH-rapha*—"the Lord who heals you"	Exodus 15:26
b. Healing in the atonement	Isaiah 53:5
c. Promise of healing	James 5:14–15
d. Gifts of healing	1 Corinthians 12:9
6. The Lord is Victory	
a. *YHWH-nissi*—"the Lord is my Banner"	Exodus 17:15
b. Promise of victory	Jeremiah 29:11
c. Source of victory: Jesus	Philippians 4:13
d. Freedom from failure	Galatians 3:13
e. "No weapon forged against you will prevail"	Isaiah 54:17
7. The Lord is Peace	
a. *YHWH-shalom*—"the Lord is Peace:	Judges 6:24
b. The peace of God: wholeness, harmony, well-being, contentment, satisfaction, blessing	Numbers 6:24–27
c. The source of peace: Jesus	Isaiah 53:5; Ephesians 2:14
d. The blessing of God	Genesis 12:3; Galatians 3:14
e. The covenants of God: salvation, sonship, blessing, provision, prosperity	Ephesians 2:12–13

PRAYER NOTEBOOK	
Topic	**Scriptures**
C. Thanksgiving for His nature	
1. Character: holy, righteous, just, infinite, eternal, omnipotent, omnipresent, omniscient, sovereign, wise	
2. Heart: loving, merciful, gracious, kind, caring, good	
III. Appropriating Divine Intervention: *"Thy Kingdom Come"*	Matthew 6:10
A. In my life—"What do I want?"	James 4:2
1. Blessing of God	Numbers 6:24–26
2. Intimacy with God (love, face, voice, vision)	Exodus 3:6
3. Pleasing to God	Psalms 19:14
a. Character: prosper and empower	Romans 8:29
b. Fruitfulness: abiding/dependence	John 15:1—5
c. Stature and maturity	Ephesians 4:13
d. Love	1 Corinthians 13
e. Availability	Isaiah 6:8
f. Leading	Psalms 25:9
4. Program of God	
a. My powerlessness	Romans 7:18
b. God's power	Matthew 28:18
c. Relinquishment: "Thy will be done"	Matthew 6:10
d. Moral inventory	Psalms 139:23–24
e. Intervention to correct defects	Psalms 51:10
f. Will to obey	John 14:21

PRAYER NOTEBOOK	
Topic	**Scriptures**
5. Kingdom of God	
a. Righteousness, peace, and joy	Romans 14:17
b. Fullness of the Holy Spirit	Ephesians 5:18
c. Kingdom, health and prosperity	3 John 2
d. Kingdom identity	Ephesians 2:6
B. In my family: ". . . Come . . . Be Done . . ."	
1. Allison: Bless, prosper, protect	
a. "Crown of beauty, oil of gladness, garment of praise"	Isaiah 61:3
b. Friends and helpers	James 4:2
c. Kingdom worth (queen of our house)	Psalms 31
d. Hearing and hormones	Exodus 15:26
e. Come upon our marriage	Ephesians 5:25
f. Relationship with Baker and Stephanie (patience, grace, love kindness, firmness)	Ephesians 6:4
2. Stephanie: Bless, prosper, protect	
a. Plans and purposes	
b. Inner purity	Psalms 144:12
c. Well-rounded growth	Luke 2:52
d. Keep undefiled	
e. Become a woman of God	Psalms 102:28
f. Special needs	
3. Baker: Bless, prosper, protect	
a. Health, nurture, strength, peace	Psalms 144:12
b. Man of God: diplomat of the kingdom	Psalms 102:28

PRAYER NOTEBOOK	
Topic	**Scriptures**
c. Kingdom kid	Luke 2:52
d. Special needs	
4. Show me their "way"	Proverbs 22:6
5. Glorify Yourself in our family	
C. In the church "... Come ... Be Done"	Matthew 16:18
1. Bless, prosper, protect, use	
2. Staff: Jim, Matt, Dutch, Tom, Schultz	1 Timothy 5:17
3. Elders: Harold, Martha Del, Rich, Mel, Jim, Gary F., Bill, Gary W., John, Paul, Curt	1 Peter 5:2–3
4. Renewal, revival, reformation	Revelation 3:8
5. The harvest: 100,000; 50,000	Acts 2:47
6. Build up the body	Ephesians 4:13
7. Make known the plan	Micah 7:11
8. Provide a place	Psalms 132:7
9. If pleasing to you: breakthrough; power-point; net to catch; weapon forged for God.	Acts 4:31
D. In the world	John 3:16
1. Our nation: mercy, forgiveness, healing	2 Chronicles 7:14
a. City: revival (Detroit—breakthrough)	Daniel 9:18
b. State: Terry C.	1 Timothy 2:1–2
c. Nation: President Bush, Bill A.	1 Timothy 2:1–2
d. Revival	Acts 4:29–30
e. Stop abortion and pornography	
2. The World:	Matthew 28:18–20
a. World hunger, world peace	1 John 3:17

PRAYER NOTEBOOK	
Topic	**Scriptures**
b. World evangelization by 2000	Matthew 24:14
c. Germany	Matthew 24:14
d. Estonia	Matthew 24:14
e. India: P. G., Josh, Paul, George	Matthew 24:14
f. France: Wes and Gerti	Matthew 24:14
g. Africa: Leroy and Kathy	Matthew 24:14
Maranatha!	1 Corinthians 16:22
IV. Praying for Provision: *"Give Us This Day . . ."*	Matthew 6:11
A. Daily needs	
1. Financial provision—Give that I can give.	2 Corinthians 8:8
2. Kingdom prosperity and success	Joshua 1:8
3. Help me meet the conditions of provision	Proverbs 3:9
a. In the will of God	Romans 12:1–2
b. In the Word and prayer	John 15:7
c. Diligent, balanced work habits	Proverbs 12:11
d. Faithful giving	Malachi 3:10
4. Daily tasks	Psalms 37:5
B. Special needs	
1. Refreshed, renewed, nurtured on Sabbath	
C. Wants and sources of anxiety	Philippians 4:6–7
1. Sale of house	Psalms 106:15
2. Car situation	Psalms 103:5
3. Vacation	Psalms 147:14
4. Responsible savings	Proverbs 10:24

PRAYER NOTEBOOK	
Topic	**Scriptures**
5. Stephanie and Baker's college education	Matthew 7:11
6. Clothing	Luke 11:13
7. Food	Psalms 35:27
8. Retirement	Psalms 128:2
9. Giving	Luke 6:38
10. Books—written and published	John 14:13–14
11. Sabbatical	John 16:24
12. Friends	Psalms 144:13
13. Fellowship	Matthew 6:33
V. Experiencing Forgiveness: *"Forgive Us Our Sins"*	Matthew 6:12
A. Confession	1 John 1:9
1. I am a sinner constantly in need of Your grace and forgiveness	Romans 3:23
2. Help remove the defects of my character:	James 5:16
a. Restless—replace with peace	Colossians 3:15
b. Irritable—replace with joy	Nehemiah 8:10
c. Discontented—replace with thanksgiving	1 Thessalonians 5:18
3. Help put to death the deeds of the flesh: lust, greed, rage, meanness, self-centeredness, harshness, insecurity, envy	Romans 8:13 Ephesians 5:3–5
4. Search me, Holy Spirit	Psalms 139:23
B. Forgiveness	Matthew 6:14
1. Lord, help me treat every offense against me today with forgiveness	Luke 23:34

PRAYER NOTEBOOK	
Topic	**Scriptures**
2. Help me remember bitterness doesn't hurt the other person, it only hurts me	Ephesians 4:31
3. Show me anyone I need to forgive	Psalms 139:23
VI. Spiritual Protection: *"Deliver Us"*	Matthew 6:13
A. Lead us not into temptation	
1. Personal holiness	1 Peter 1:16
2. Armor of God	Ephesians 6:13
3. Biblical humility	James 4:6
4. Spiritual authority	Ephesians 2:6
B. Deliver us from the evil one	
1. Spiritual "hedge"	Job 1:10
2. Refuge, fortress, shield, rampart	Psalms 5:11–12
3. Presence and power	Psalms 91:1–4
4. Host of heaven	Hebrews 1:14
VII. Final Issues: *"Yours Is"*	Matthew 6:13
A. The kingdom—let me live a kingdom life today	Luke 12:32
B. The power—strengthen me with power in my inner man	Ephesians 3:16
C. The glory—glorify Yourself through my life today	2 Corinthians 3:18
Amen	
Intercession	
A. Friends in Ministry	
1. Rich: Doulos	
2. Jeff: K. C. Vineyard	
3. Bob and Ted: Colonial	
4. Mike: K. C. F.	

PRAYER NOTEBOOK	
Topic	**Scriptures**
5. Denny: Coast Hills	
6. Stan and Debbie: Downing House	
B. Neighbors	
1. Ken and Leslie	
2. John and Pam	
3. Barb and Hartley	
4. Michael and Dawn	
5. Mike and Susan	
6. Tom and Carolyn	
7. Bill and Pam	
8. John and Nancy	
9. Rich and Betty	
10. Howard and Dorsey	
C. Ministries	
1. Heart of a Champion	
2. Tuesday mornings: Band of Brothers	
3. Sunday mornings: the harvest	
4. Wednesday nights: Company of the Committed	
D. Friends	
1. Bevans Branham	
2. Steve Combs	
3. Mike Schaeffer	
4. Chuck Berling	
5. Tad Polumbus	
6. Bob Skold	
7. Bill Wall	

PRAYER NOTEBOOK	
Topic	**Scriptures**
8. Gary McGill	
9. Kim Ellick	
10. Eddie Suharski	
11. Rich Valenciano	
12. Tom Weins	
13. Craig Hartshorn	
Miracle List	Ephesians 3:20
Impossible apart from intervention by the living God	Jeremiah 33:3
1. Bo and Gari	Psalms 114:8
2. 100,000—South Denver—90s	Psalms 115:3
3. Chad's leg	
4. Susan's baby	
5. Megan's healing	
6. Requests too confidential for public revelation.	
7. "	
8. "	
9. "	
10. "	
11. "	
12. "	
13. "	

DEVELOPING YOUR PRAYER NOTEBOOK

PRAYER NOTEBOOK	
Topic	**Scriptures**
I. Entering His Presence: "Father . . ."	

PRAYER NOTEBOOK	
Topic	**Scriptures**
II. Seeking His Face: "Hallowed be Your Name"	

PRAYER NOTEBOOK	
Topic	Scriptures
III. Appropriating Divine Intervention: "Thy kingdom come . . ."	

PRAYER NOTEBOOK	
Topic	**Scriptures**
IV. Praying for Provision: "Give us this day . . ."	

PRAYER NOTEBOOK	
Topic	Scriptures
V. Experiencing Forgiveness: "Forgive us our sins . . ."	

PRAYER NOTEBOOK	
Topic	Scriptures
VI. Spiritual Protection: "Deliver us from the evil one. . . ."	

PRAYER NOTEBOOK	
Topic	Scriptures
VII. Final Issues: "Yours is . . ."	

SUBJECT INDEX

SCRIPTURE INDEX

ABOUT THE AUTHOR

Bob Beltz is the Executive Pastor of Cherry Hills Community Church in Englewood, Colorado. For the last ten years he has been part of the leadership team that has seen the church grow from a handful of men to one of the fastest growing churches in America. Bob and his wife Allison moved to Colorado in 1975 to attend Denver Conservative Baptist Seminary where Bob earned both his Master of Arts and Doctor of Ministry degrees.

As Executive Pastor, Bob's primary role has been to utilize his gifts in the area of teaching and leadership. His Wednesday evening Bible study averages one thousand men and women who come together as "The Company of the Committed." Bob also teaches a weekly men's Bible study of three hundred businessmen from the Denver community.

Bob and Allison have a daughter, Stephanie, who is eleven and a son, Baker, who is five. Bob has also published a layman's commentary on the book of Revelation entitled *How to Survive the End of the World,* and currently has several other writing projects in process.

The typeface for the text of this book is *Palatino*. This type—best known as a contemporary *italic* typeface—was a post-World War II design crafted by the talented young German calligrapher Hermann Zapf. For inspiration, Zapf drew upon the writing legacy of a group of Italian Renaissance writing masters, in which the typeface's namesake, Giovanni Battista Palatino, was numbered. Giovanni Palatino's *Libro nuovo d'imparare a scrivera* was published in Rome in 1540 and became one of the most used, wide-ranging writing manuals of the sixteenth century. Zapf was an apt student of the European masters, and contemporary *Palatino* is one of his contributions to modern typography.

Substantive Editing:
Michael S. Hyatt

Copy Editing:
Donna Walter Sherwood

Cover Design:
Steve Diggs & Friends
Nashville, Tennessee

Page Composition:
Xerox Ventura Publisher
Linotronic L-100 Postscript® Imagesetter

Printing and Binding:
Maple-Vail Book Manufacturing Group
York, Pennsylvania

Cover Printing:
Strine Printing Company
York, Pennsylvania